D0266046

by the same author

NICK BROOMFIELD: DOCUMENTING ICONS

The Faber Book of Mexican Cinema

Jason Wood

faber and faber

First published in 2006
by Faber and Faber Limited
Bloomsbury House
74-77 Great Russell Street
London WC1B 3DA

Typeset by Refinecatch Limited, Bungay, Suffolk

Printed and bound in Great Britain by
CPI Antony Rowe, Chippenham and Eastbourne

A CIP record for this book
is available from the British Library

ISBN 978-0-571-21732-8
ISBN 0-571-21732-x

Contents

Illustrations

Interviews

Carlos Reygadas, Director: 17 August 2002, London
Alfonso Cuarón, Director: 21 November 2002, London
Carlos Cuarón, Writer/Director: 8 August 2003, Mexico
Emmanuel Lubezki, Cinematographer: 14 July 2003, Mexico
Bertha Navarro, Producer: 30 September 2003, Mexico City
Ángeles Castro, Director of The Centro de Capacitación Cinematográfica: 1 October 2003, Mexico City
Laura Imperiale, Producer: 2 October 2003, Mexico City
Guillermo Arriaga, Writer: 2 October 2003, Mexico City
Francisco González Compeán, Producer: 3 October 2003, Mexico City
Alfredo Joskowicz, Director of IMCINE: 3 October 2003, Mexico City
Martha Sosa, Producer: 4 October 2003, Mexico City
Carlos Carrera, Director: 4 October 2003, Mexico City
Leonardo García Tsao, Critic/Academic: 15 October 2003, Mexico City
Alejandro González Iñárritu, Director: 1 November 2003, London
Rosa Bosch, Producer: 7 November 2003, London
Juan Carlos Rulfo, Director: 8 November 2003, Mexico City
Brigitte Broch, Production Designer: 8 November 2003, New York
Daniel Birman, Producer: 21 November 2003, Mexico City
Guillermo del Toro, Director: 24 November 2003 Los Angeles
Rodrigo Prieto, Cinematographer: 14 December 2003, London
Salvador Carrasco, Director: 15 December 2003, Los Angeles
Martín Salinas, Writer: 29 December 2003, Buenos Aires
Hugo Rodríguez, Director: 13 January 2004
Gael García Bernal, Actor: 14 January 2004, New York
José Luis García Agraz, Director: 20 January 2004 Mexico City

Introduction

> It's chemistry, alchemy, pieces falling together at the same time. How can you effectively explain other essential moments in film history, like the German New Wave? Sometimes these things are just moments in time, linked to specific political, social or cultural situations. It's not only that there were a bunch of film-makers. There were also actors, cinematographers, production designers, producers . . .
>
> Rosa Bosch, producer, *The Devil's Backbone*

Enjoying phenomenal critical and commercial success in quick succession, *Amores Perros* and *Y tu mamá también* alerted the eyes of the world to the riches to be found in Mexican cinema. The former marked the audacious directorial debut of Alejandro González Iñárritu; the latter was the work of Alfonso Cuarón, a more experienced film-maker returning home for a personal project, after a fruitful Hollywood excursion. Both films featured the poster-boy looks and electrifying screen presence of Gael García Bernal; each was confident, stylishly shot and structurally complex. Moreover, these films were thematically provocative in their treatment of prescient social issues, and thrillingly forthright in their willingness to address the ills afflicting contemporary Mexican society.

The global media, ever eager to pinpoint a new trend, wasted little time in devoting many column inches to predicting an exciting new wave, or *buena onda*, and Mexican cinema immediately became its darling. However, a more informed assessment of film production in Mexico, largely through the pages of industry periodicals such as *Screen International* and *Variety*, soon revealed a harsher and somewhat paradoxical reality; and in turn the headlines just as quickly became epitaphs. Attention shifted to Argentina – a country reeling from economic collapse – and yet still able to sustain a profitable cinema industry and nurture the careers of emerging talents such as Pablo Trapero (*El Bonaerense*, 2002, and *Familia Rodante*, 2006) and Lucrecia Martel (*La Ciénaga*, 2001, and *La Niña Santa*, 2004).

On the one hand there existed an undeniable surplus of young, formally daring creative talent, whose rise to prominence coincided with an emerging generation of Mexican cinema-goers thirsting for intelligent, identity-affirming, locally made product. Having endured a period of relative famine throughout the 1980s and for much of the early 1990s, Mexican audiences had, for the most part, given up on Mexican cinema, preferring instead to pay to see the numerous American productions that were filling the screens at the increasingly popular multiplex cinemas springing up throughout the country. Now, though, they once more had a national cinema to be optimistic about, one that matched if not bettered the films imported from across the border; a cinema with its own stars, its own high production values, and its own characters and concerns. These Mexican audiences were once again able to recognize themselves, their hopes, aspirations and troubles, on screen.

Facilitating the aspirations of film-makers and audiences alike was a new entrepreneurial spirit among private investors and producers, a good number of whom had valiantly struggled under the closed-shop mentality of previous administrations, taking the crumbs that fell occasionally from the table of the state-controlled industry. Prepared to invest time, energy and money on unconventional projects that were not, in the majority of instances, mere local variations on American genre pictures, they soon understood that financial autonomy from the existing government institutions also accorded formal and ideological liberty. No subject was taboo, no narrative too complex, in the continued search for an authentic means of expression and the need to address directly the ever-present issue of what it meant to be Mexican.

Conversely, and severely undermining these outwardly fertile conditions, was the unfavourable distribution of the peso at the box office, a distribution that made recouping costs for private producers almost impossible. Without government-initiated tax incentives, and confronted by escalating production costs and prints and advertising budgets, private producers faced an arduous task even getting an independent feature off the ground. With the eyes of the world looking on, it became all too apparent that the Mexican cinema industry was beset by structural problems so deep rooted and irreparable that they threatened to place a foot to the throat of what had briefly been a tantalizing renaissance.

This book – compounded of extensive interviews with a rich diversity of leading lights and industry professionals, edited into a narrative interspersed with linking prose – is an attempt to offer a clear perspective on the current aesthetic and economic climate, while also contextualizing contemporary Mexican cinema in relation to its own frequently brilliant but equally troubled past. By the same token, a film such as *Amores Perros* did not emerge from a vacuum and so it is essential that *Contemporary Mexican Cinema* touch on some of its key antecedents and the social, political, technical and individual and collective creative forces that helped give birth to it.

A constantly shifting environment confronts today's Mexican film-industry professionals. The clearest and most alarming example of this is the now thwarted plans of Mexican President, Vicente Fox, to extinguish state involvement in cinema by closing the Mexican Film Institute (IMCINE), calling time on Mexico's leading film school, the Centro de Capacitación Cinematográfica (the institution that trained many of the people with whom I spoke), and selling off for real-estate-development purposes the legendary Studios Churubusco.

The howls of outrage that greeted Fox's proposals – proposals that were perceived as direct attacks on culture and identity and that would remove the last barriers to American cultural domination – is evidence of the strength of spirit and the feeling of community within the Mexican cinema fraternity. Just as González Iñárritu, Alfonso Cuarón and Guillermo del Toro – the directors perhaps most popularly associated with recent Mexican cinema, whose high profiles have seen them assume ambassadorial roles – are all close friends and frequent advisers on each other's works. This sense of kinship, encouragement and responsibility has helped to sustain Mexican cinema in times both good and bad.

Viva México!

Jason Wood

I

'Golden Age', *El Grupo Nuevo Cine*, Boom and Bust

ALFONSO CUARÓN *director*: Remember what Claude Chabrol said: 'There is no wave, there is only the ocean.' I am not purely interested in 'Mexican cinema', I am interested in cinema. And when you start using these words like 'wave', it's a way of creating an identity for certain films, but it also becomes an aspect of marketing. You know, the common identity of the films people are describing as part of this 'Mexican wave' is that they are from Mexico, but the only other thing they have in common is that they are cinema. And that is the reason these films are seen everywhere and why they have been embraced everywhere. But people are also disregarding Mexican film-makers who have been making films for the last thirty years – people like Arturo Ripstein. You have to remember that there have been lots of Mexican film directors, but that doesn't make a 'wave' – it's not as if we have all shared a particular aesthetic.

HUGO RODRÍGUEZ *director*: Let's not forget that Mexico has a long film-making tradition, which started almost at the same time as the international film industry was born. We have films that date back to the early 1900s, and the historical relationship with Hollywood has meant that our technicians are highly trained.

One of the belle époque*'s success stories, Mexico was prosperous and politically stable in the 1890s. It should come as little surprise, then, that the movie projectors and early films produced by the Lumière Brothers should appear there shortly after they became popular in Europe. Mexican audiences greeted the new form of entertainment just as enthusiastically as had their European counterparts; and, while it is not well documented, there was certainly a 'silent-film era' in Mexico, with the origins of cinema there linked to Salvador Toscano Barragán, an engineering student who opened the first Mexican movie salon and began to create some of the country's first film productions. By 1900 the popularity of cinema within Mexico – and particularly Mexico City – was well established, with new salons opening and new equipment being imported.*

In this formative period the majority of 'entertainments' were locally produced documentations of momentous national events, such as the opening of new railway lines and presidential excursions. However, in 1908 one of the first major films to be produced from a script was completed: Felipe de Jesús's El Grito de Dolores. *After a period of boom, there followed one of decline in the 1920s as Hollywood established itself as the dominant force in film-making. With audiences turning increasingly to imported newsreels originating from America, film production in Mexico – which was not supported by the state – suffered a rapid downturn, while the more sophisticated Hollywood films successfully offered fantasy and escape. This rejection of localized product would repeat itself many times. Moreover, such Mexican film artists as had established themselves were not adverse to overtures from the north, and so figures such as Delores del Río and Lupita Tovar set sail for pastures new.*

It was the coming of sound that allowed Mexico to regain ground as a film-making entity, and although in 1932 (a few years after the important arrival of Sergei Eisenstein in the country) only six films were produced, two were by directors who would make a valuable contribution to the country's cinema: Fernando de Fuentes (El anónimo) *and Soviet émigré Arcady Boytler* (Mano a mano). *Buoyed by renewed private investment (for example, wealthy distributor Juan de la Cruz Alarcón formed the Compañía Nacional Productora de Películas), Mexican cinema was once again at the forefront of Spanish-language film production by 1933.*

LEONARDO GARCÍA TSAO *critic/academic*: 'The History of Mexican Cinema' is a course I have not yet taught and, to be honest, it's not something that I would really enjoy teaching – although there are some Mexican films that I enjoy very much, by the likes of Emilio Fernández and Fernando de Fuentes.

A former actor who in the 1920s found work in the United States, Emilio Fernández returned to Mexico and leading-man status with roles in Carlos Navarro's Janitzio *(1934) and Rafael E. Portas's* Adiós Nicanor *(1937). In 1941 Fernández made his directorial debut with* La isla de la pasión. *Two years later Fernández teamed up with actors Delores del Río and Pedro Armendáriz on projects such as* Flor Silvestre *and* María Candelaria. *Winning numerous festival prizes and bringing Mexican cinema to wider international attention, Fernández directed well into the 1970s, completing his final work,* Erótica, *in 1978.*

Fernando de Fuentes began his career as a cinema manager, and would later use his experience in this regard to challenge the existing exhibition monopoly of the 1940s. He became arguably the most important figure in the Mexican cinema of the 1930s because of his trilogy of films about the Revolution: El prisionere trece *(1933),* El compadre Mendoza *(1933) and* Vámonos con Pancho Villa *(1934).*

Emerging from this period is what is termed 'The Golden Age of Mexican Cinema', or 'El Cine de Oro'. It coincided with the administration of Miguel Alemán between the years 1946 and 1952, and was inextricably linked to unprecedented economic growth and prosperity, proving to be a high point both in terms of production (quantity as well as quality) and of profits. A major contributing factor to Mexico's film-making status at this time was the courting of Mexico as a valuable ally against Axis countries by the US. Increased revenue and access to technology became widely available. Similarly, the period saw an increased attention to film-making by the state as it sought to protect what was becoming a valuable cultural and economic asset. Thus, in 1942, the Banco Nacional Cinematográfica was founded to facilitate the funding of film production. A law was also passed in 1946 that protected the film industry from income tax: 'Thriving in the shade of the state's protection and subsidization, Mexican cinema found itself in the midst of a Golden Age, an era of quality films and high output that continued into the late 1950s.'[1] It was also through these movies that a romanticized and idealized view of Mexico was projected on to movie screens across Latin America, giving Mexico a dominance in this market second only to Hollywood.

Though born in Spain, Luis Buñuel – widely credited as the founder of surrealist cinema with films such as Un Chien andalou *(made with Salvador Dalí, 1929) and* L'Age d'Or *(1930) – is inextricably linked to the development of Mexican cinema and remains one of its most prominent and influential figures. Emerging at the tail end of the 'Cine de Oro' period, the director arguably provides a lineage with the subsequent 'Grupo Nuevo Cine', and – through his unsentimental consideration of themes of poverty and social injustice, allied with his formal experimentation and ability to work creatively with limited resources – to the prominent Mexican directors who would emerge on the cusp of the twenty-first century.*

Having, like many Spanish artists and intellectuals, relocated to Mexico in 1946 following the Spanish Civil War (becoming a Mexican citizen in 1949), Buñuel embarked on Gran Casino *(also known as* En el viejo Tampico, *1947), his first directorial project since 1933's* Las Hurdes.

[1] Berg, *Cinema of Solitude*, p. 15.

Working extensively with producer Óscar Dancigers, Buñuel would go on to produce a number of Mexican films including Los olvidados *(1950),* El *(1953),* Ensayo de un crimen *(1955) and* Nazarín *(1959) and* Viridiana *(1961). That last picture once again garnered him international attention and acclaim, precipitating a return to international productions such as* Belle du Jour *(1967) and* Tristana *(1970). Though working mostly in France during the latter part of his career, Buñuel would return frequently to his adopted Mexican homeland, eventually dying in Mexico City in 1983.*

GUILLERMO DEL TORO *director*: Goya is one of my favourite painters, and I think that Goya didn't really come to be until the last days of his life when he produced his 'Black Paintings'.[2] That is the ultimate expression of him. The same with Alfred Hitchcock – I think that the only real glimpse of the very dark and very complex man that Alfred Hitchcock was comes with watching *Frenzy* (1972). To my mind the opposite happened with Buñuel. I think that Buñuel did some of his best work very early on, and then went to read what the critics had to say about him and started to make movies that were a little too hermetic. I maintain that his Mexican period is his best period.

LEONARDO GARCÍA TSAO: There were one or two good Mexican films in the 1960s but, with the exception of Buñuel, the movie scene was pretty poor then. So people of that generation developed and sustained a prejudice against Mexican films. It was a class thing. The upper-middle classes deemed that watching Mexican movies didn't befit their social position: they felt that only the lower classes would go to see such films. I remember, when I was a kid, my father would resolutely say, 'No way! We are *not* going to see a Mexican movie!'

Identified in 1960 after a series of concerts attended by leftists critics, scholars and film-makers including Buñuel, El Grupo Nuevo Cine published the magazine Nuevo Cine *from April 1960 to August 1962. A manifesto criticizing the state of the Mexican film industry,* Nuevo Cine *demanded a number of sweeping reforms, including the formation of an institution to teach film-making, and increased exhibition and production of independent films.*

[2] Goya's 'Black Paintings' were completed while the artist was living in seclusion outside of Madrid. Extremely personal in style – and executed on his walls – the fourteen paintings gave expression to his deepest and darkest visions.

LEONARDO GARCÍA TSAO: From the *Nuevo Cine* magazine came the idea that Mexican cinema really had to change, and so they organized an experimental film contest.

In part a response to declining production levels, but also as a response to calls from young university-based cineastes, the leading Mexican film union, the Sindicato de Trabajadores de la Producción Cinematográfica, announced the First Contest of Experimental Cinema in 1964. Founded in 1919 as the Unión de Empleados Confederados del Cinematográfica, the STPC *was the union that by 1944 came to represent all film workers.*

The entries were judged in July 1965 by a thirteen-person panel, representing the industry, critics and cultural institutions. First prize was awarded to Rubén Gámez's La fórmula secreta *(*The Secret Formula*, 1965), a surrealistic work dealing with Mexico's search for identity. Second prize was awarded to Alberto Isaac's* En este pueblo no hay ladrones *(*In This Town There Are No Thieves*, 1964).*

JUAN CARLOS RULFO *director*: Rubén Gámez, for whom I worked as assistant director, I regard as the most inventive film director Mexico has had in the last forty years, and the one who has taken the most risks. His films *Megueyes* (1962), *La fórmula secreta* (*The Secret Formula*, 1965), and *Tequila* (1992), among others, are points of reference for anyone wishing to talk about the roots of Mexican and experimental cinema.

JOSÉ LUIS GARCÍA AGRAZ *director*: At sixteen, I wanted to be a professional footballer, a guitarist in a rock band, a poet, a cartoonist, and a heroic guerrilla fighter. That was 1968, and the government was brutally putting down any attempt to make society more democratic. Teachers, doctors and railway workers were murdered, put in prison; it was a period that ended with the cruel suppression of the student movement on 2 October in Tlatelolco to the north of Mexico City, which was a place of Aztec sacrifice before the arrival of the Spanish in the sixteenth century; then a shunting yard in the 1920s, and a middle-class housing project in the early 1970s.

Following mass outbreaks of anti-government demonstrations across the country during the summer of 1968, some six thousand students and non-student protestors (including women and children) gathered on 2 October 1968 at the Plaza of the Three Cultures in Tlatelolco. Government troops opened fire on the protestors (the government was to later protest that students had fired first), killing an estimated two hundred people and wounding hundreds more.

The generation that cut their teeth in 1968 duly rose to the forefront in the 1970s and collectively brought about an important cinematic movement.

LEONARDO GARCÍA TSAO: The 1970s brought a slight change, with Felipe Cazals and Arturo Ripstein. I was a student at university then, and this was the time when I started to get interested in watching Mexican films. I remember that in class we would all decide to go see the new film by Cazals or Ripstein.

Born in France, Felipe Cazals had lived in Mexico since early childhood. Originally working in Mexican television and later on a number of short films for the film department of Belles Artes, Cazals directed his first feature in 1968, the independently produced La manzana de la discordia *(*The Apple of Discord*). As a reaction against the difficulties of breaking into the national film industry, in 1969 Cazals collaborated with Arturo Ripstein, Rafael Castenado and Pedro F. Miret to create the influential if short-lived Cine Independiente de Mexico group. Subsequently working with state funding on numerous high-scale productions (*El Jardín de tía Isabel*, 1971, and* Aquellos años*, 1972, among them), Cazals began to focus more and more on projects concerned with highlighting the social and ethnic problems affecting Mexico. 1975's* Canoa *(written by Tomás Perez Turrent), a documentary-style examination of a 1968 uprising by a Mexico City student movement, is perhaps his best-known work.*

ALFONSO CUARÓN: When I was growing up and realized I wanted to make films, there were directors who showed me there were other approaches to the cheesy sex comedies that were being produced in Mexico. A very important film for me was *Canoa* by Felipe Cazals.

The winner of a Special Jury Prize at the Berlin Film Festival, Canoa *recreates the real-life events of 1968 in which four employees of the University of Puebla were lynched by the townspeople of San Miguel de Canoa. Based on a script by film critic Tomás Pérez Turrent,* Canoa's *documentary aesthetic was much imitated and the film is widely regarded as a classic of the national cinema.*

Cazals was subsequently to fall in and out of favour with the national cinema industry and his post–1970s output is largely made up of less personal projects and generic pictures undertaken on commission.

Born in Mexico City in 1943, Arturo Ripstein, son of producer Alfredo Ripstein jnr, had been involved in the Mexican film industry since childhood. After appearing in supporting roles in the 1960s, Ripstein worked as an assistant to Luis Buñuel on The Exterminating Angel *(1962). At the age of twenty-one Ripstein adapted a script by Gabriel García Márquez to make his feature debut,* Tiempo de Morir *(1965). A director of truly international standing whose work has been celebrated at festivals worldwide, Ripstein's key films include* El castillo de la pureza *(1972);* El Santo oficio *(1973); and* El lugar sin límites *(1977).*

*Two other substantive film-makers of the 1970s were Jorge Fons and Alfredo Joskowicz. Fons, part of the first graduation class of the Centro Universatario de Estudios Cinematográficos (*CUEC*), was initially an assistant director to Arturo Ripstein before moving into directing 'telenovelas' on Mexican television and establishing his own directorial career. Fons's early work includes the* Caridad *segment of* Fe, esperanza y caridad *(1972) and* Los albañiles *(1976).*

Beginning his film-making career with 1968's La Manda, *Alfredo Joskowicz is widely considered to have made two of the finest Mexican films of the early 1970s in* Crates *(1970) and* El Cambio *(*The Change, *1971). Made in the wake of the massacre at Tlatelolco, both films echoed an acute disillusionment with Mexican society.*

*An institutional strength was added to Mexican cinema in the 1970s through the presidency (*sexenio*) of Luis Echeverría Álvarez. Coming to power in 1970, Institutional Revolutionary Party (*PRI*) candidate Echeverría regarded cinema as a tool through which Mexico could be promoted throughout the world. Throughout his* sexenio *(1970–76) Echeverría was extremely supportive of cinema, offering a state level of financial and infrastructural backing that provided an exciting opportunity for emerging film-makers.*

ALFREDO JOSKOWICZ, *film-maker/Director,* IMCINE: At the beginning of the 1970s there was a very new look to Mexican cinema, but this arose from the decision of the government to make film-making more democratic. Previously, the Banco Nacional Cinematográfico had given money for film production only to a very narrow and business-orientated band of independent film producers, and Echeverría abolished this system. He installed his brother Rodolfo[3] as the head of the BNC and sanctioned the establishing of

[3] A former president of Asociación Nacional de Actores (ANDA), Rodolfo Echeverría (screen name Rodolfo Landa) was a well-known actor in Mexican cinema.

three state-formed production companies: CONACINE, CONACITE I and CONACITE II. To ensure a consistency of quality, the state became the major film producer in Mexico. But it was not a conservative film-making environment – the opposite, in fact, it was a time of liberal ideological reform.

Echeverría also ensured that the two major films studios, including Estudios America and Estudios Churubusco – where I also worked for the last four years before coming to IMCINE – became the base for Mexican film production. Echeverría also created the Centro de Capacitación Cinematográfica and generally ensured a heightened commitment to exhibiting and distributing locally produced cinema. Cinema was very almost – but not quite totally – an entirely state-funded and controlled industry. So the state effectively held control of production, distribution and exhibition.

Echeverría established a relaxed and liberating film-making environment where the emphasis was not on turning a quick buck by churning out production after production but rather on quality, diversity and freedom of speech. An explosion of internationally acclaimed film-making ensued, in which directors such as Cazals, Ripstein, Miguel Littín, Jaime Humberto Hermosillo, and Paul Leduc – considered part of the New Cinema movement – rose to prominence.

After studying film-making at IDHEC *in Paris, Mexico City-born Paul Leduc returned to Mexico in 1967 and directed seventeen documentary shorts for the Olympic Committee with Cine 70, a group he had helped found alongside Rafael Castanedo, Alexis Grivas and Bertha Navarro.*

BERTHA NAVARRO *producer*: I directed theatre productions at university when I was younger and then I graduated to directing short films. I originally studied anthropology and was going to become an anthropologist, but then I became enraptured by documentary cinema and decided to get involved. I met Paul Leduc and cinematographer Alexis Grivas; both had studied at IDHEC in Paris and had just come back to Mexico and so we decided to work together. Then came the Olympic Games and we had a lot of work, so I started to help out even more by producing and even editing some of the films.

Leduc's work would be characterized by a high degree of political commitment, and he truly came to prominence with Reed: México Insurgente *(*Reed: Insurgent Mexico, *1973), a historical work with the aesthetics of a documentary, based on American journalist John Reed's account of the Mexican Revolution.*

BERTHA NAVARRO: Paul and I did our first feature film together, *Reed: México Insurgente*, when I was twenty-six. I acted in the film and also produced it. It was an independent film and a huge adventure. The industry and the unions were so closed that they wouldn't let anybody new in, and so we were forced to take the independent route. I've worked in different moments of this industry, and it has *always* been about challenging and breaking the structures that don't allow you to do things.

We were called 'pirates'. We were a young generation trying to do new things within the older structure of the Mexican film industry. *Reed: México Insurgente* was actually promoted by the official industry institutions, who sent it to numerous international festivals. We also had a huge amount of backing from intellectuals and the cultural community within Mexico – Carlos Fuentes cited it as one of the best films he'd seen. With all this backing and support the existing structures tried to integrate us into their system, and we went to Cannes, where the film was selected for the Directors' Fortnight. It made a big impact, and so we decided to take our 16 mm print and have it blown up to 35 mm. This was also done with the help of the industry officials. It was a good start for us, but after the film nothing really changed, because the industry officials didn't wish to help us make another project, and they certainly weren't going to provide any financial aid.

LEONARDO GARCÍA TSAO: The 1970s, the Echeverría period, saw the cinematic fruits of the Nuevo Cine group, which in the 1960s had been purely theoretical.

ALFREDO JOSKOWICZ: It's a very long list of film-makers who flourished but one that would certainly include Jaime Humberto Hermosillo, Alfonso Arau, Gonzalo Martínez and Alberto Isaac. I was the previous generation: we were aggressive, but the industry was completely closed to us.

A student of the Centro Universatario de Estudios Cinematográficos (CUEC), Jaime Humberto Hermosillo made his full-feature commercial debut with La verdarera vocación de Magdalena *(1971). His subsequent career alternated between highly personal projects that examine issues of class, gender and sexuality, and more lacklustre, overtly commercial fare. In the 1980s, generally considered to be Hermosillo's weakest period, his films garnered a cult international following, specifically* Doña Herlinda y su hijo *(*Doña Herlinda and Her Son, *1984), regarded as the first openly gay film in the history of Mexican cinema.*

Alfonso Arau's films include: El Águila descalza *(*The Barefoot Eagle,

1969), Calzonzin Inspector *(*Inspector Calzonzin, *1973),* Mojado Power *(1979) and, most famously,* Como agua para chocolate *(*Like Water for Chocolate, *1992).*

After working in documentary, Gonzalo Martínez made his feature debut with Tú, yo, nosotros *(1970), co-directed with Juan Manuel Torres and Jorge Fons.* El Principio *(1972) won numerous awards. He was prolific in film and documentary until his death in 1998.*

Alberto Isaac was a member of the Nuevo Cine group and later the first Director of IMCINE, *after having been previously blacklisted by Margarita López Portillo for publicly criticizing Mexico's investment of approximately half a million dollars in* Superman *(1978); his other credits include:* Las visitaciones del diablo *(1967);* Fútbol México *(1970);* Tívoli *(1974);* Tiempo de lobos *(1981) and* ¡Maten a Chinto! *(1989).*

For all its obvious virtues, President Echeverría's emphasis on quality inevitably led to a decline in the number of films produced annually. In 1970, the start of his presidency, eighty-two films were produced. In 1976, at its end, the number had dropped to just thirty-five.

ALFREDO JOSKOWICZ: And now we enter the tragic story of Mexican cinema. The amount of films made by private producers was decreasing while the amount of films produced by the state was increasing. The privately funded films were shot in two or three weeks, and were of extremely low quality. Remember also that in Mexico, for a very long time, the price of admittance was 40 cents, whereas in America it was about $2.50. So these privately made films were exported to the Mexican communities living in America, so that the producers could make more money.

At the end of the Echeverría period, cinema suffered a massive devaluation. The private producers said that they had to make fifty-two films per year, and they did this with the guarantee of the state that these films, though not state-funded, would be exhibited in the government-owned exhibition chain. At the beginning of 1979 the Banco Nacional Cinematográfico closed, and CONACITE I was also abolished. As a result, there began the retreat of the state from film production, and the return to prominence of the private producer.

When José López Portillo assumed power in 1976 he quickly labelled his predecessor's term a disaster, taking the view that 'fewer films meant fewer profits'.[4] *Reversing many of Echeverría's advancements and policies*

[4] Berg, *Cinema of Solitude*, p. 15.

(including dissolving CONACITE I, *reintroducing a stricter censorship, and encouraging the return of private investment and fat-cat producers to reduce the involvement of the state in the industry), Portillo's* sexenio *(1976–82) did once again see annual production levels rise (ninety-four features in 1981) but it also led to 'lowered production values and an intensified suppression of films dealing with difficult social themes'.*

*His sister Margarita López Portillo was made the Head of the Directorate of Radio, Television, and Cinema (*RTC*), a new government agency established to oversee all state-owned electronic mass media production. Preferring the term supervision to censorship, Margarita López Portillo oversaw the return to a more cautious and conservative climate.*

ALFREDO JOSKOWICZ: I was Director at the Centro de Capacitación Cinematográfia (CCC) for six years during the worst period of Margarita López Portillo. Every day Margarita was trying to close the school . . .

LEONARDO GARCÍA TSAO: The Echeverría presidency had really helped a lot of young film-makers. After Echeverría, things went really bad and people again began to stay away from the cinema. I remember Paul Leduc's *Frida* (1984) coming out and nobody going to see it. A great shame – it's much better than the Hollywood film directed by Julie Taymor.

After 1976, the generation of 1968 became marginalized. But during 1981, the penultimate year of López Portillo's sexenio, *ninety-four feature length films were produced in Mexico. Despite the conservative nature of the majority of these films (resulting from a state-supervised return to a more cautious cinema) and the fact that the bulk of them are now considered to be of variable technical quality, Mexico had attained its highest level of production since the 1950s. Margarita López Portillo was arguably justified in her claim that the administration of López Portillo had 'resurrected' Mexican film-making.*

LAURA IMPERIALE *producer*: In those days, the reality of Mexican cinema was completely different from what it is today. Production was dominated by the old-school producers and the cinematographic labour unions. In order to show a film you needed to have a film licence, and this licence was granted by the union as long as you had worked in accordance with its rules, and used its affiliates and numerous staff. The films produced were basically *gringo* films – we provided production services – and very poor quality both in terms of story and technically speaking; except for the honourable exceptions of films produced by the state for directors such as Felipe Cazals, Arturo Ripstein, Jorge Fons and a few others.

As a result of this situation there was a strong independent cinema movement, which differed from the 'industry' of the time in the subject-matter of its stories and in the way they tried to produce films. Out of this came what would later be known as the 'New Mexican Cinema'. Several of these productions were made by co-operatives and shot in Super-16, which was the way to get round the union rules.

ALFREDO JOSKOWICZ: There would almost always be something good happening still, even with the decreased amount of films produced by the state, because the ambitions were so different. The state-produced films were certainly less interested in commerce, but they were also more *outré*, if you like. You therefore had a very schizophrenic situation, as we had a handful of good films with very low commercial success and a lot of bad films that were commercially successful.

At the end of López Portillo's *sexenio* and the beginning of Miguel de la Madrid Hurtado's presidency, there was another massive devaluation of cinema. The state maintained some involvement, but only a very small amount of money was given to production and it was the export market that was privileged over any attempt to satisfy the demands of domestic cinemagoers. Films were being made at an average cost of between $100,000 and $200,000, and so the quality of the films was generally extremely poor. The films of this period were being shot and completed in as little of two weeks.

*In March 1983, Alberto Isaac was named the first Head of the newly created Mexican Film Institute (*IMCINE*), under the presidency of Miguel de la Madrid.* IMCINE*'s task was seen by Isaac to 'rebuild a ruined cinema in a ruined country'.*[5]

With the national cinema dramatically impoverished it was decided by the newly elected president that the state would need to once again become a cultural arbiter. As well as fulfilling this role, IMCINE *would also be the structure through which various other much needed sweeping reforms would be implemented and upheld. Such reforms included the dispersal of newly available state funds to film-makers; the continued insurance of prolonged employment for the country's many technicians (the privately produced films made under López Portillo might have been dreadful but they did ensure that an industry continued to exist); the encouragement of a*

[5] Mora, *Mexican Cinema: Reflections of Society*, p. 149.

wider diversity of film product in both political and aesthetic terms, and an attention to ways in which television and the mass audience it commanded might act as a facilitating organ vis-à-vis the production of more highly crafted and stimulating cinematic product.

IMCINE *would prove that the state was serious about getting its cinema industry back on track and would be the body through which a new vision for Mexican cinema could be first implemented and then sustained. Like other national cinema bodies, it would not merely exist as a bank through which grants and funding would be dispersed (though it would oversee the* FOPROCINE *(Fondo de Fomento a la Producción Cinematográfica) and* FIDECINE *funding schemes) but would be the infrastructure through which Mexican film would be able to exist once again at the interface of art, commerce, and popular entertainment.*

The selection of Alberto Isaac was a shrewd one. A much respected veteran director who had been blacklisted by the previous administration, Isaac offered the film industry hope that the state's intentions were true. Under Isaac's stewardship, there was hope among the film community that Mexican cinema – if freed from the suffocating red tape of bureaucracy that had stifled previous governmental 'interference' in localized cinema production – could once again establish its identity and reflect the culture of its people once more in cinema theatres in Mexico and throughout the world.

In this transitional moment, the 1980s did not produce a considerable yield of leading new Mexican directors. Best known among those who did emerge was Luis Mandoki from Mexico City, who made a name in his homeland before answering overtures to work in the US.

ALFONSO CUARÓN: Luis Mandoki is of a slightly different generation from myself, the one right after Arturo Ripstein. I was an assistant to Luis for many years – he's perhaps my mentor. In a way, Luis was the first Mexican director who was very comfortable working in Hollywood.

LEONARDO GARCÍA TSAO: Mandoki had really made only shorter pieces in Mexico such as *El secreto* (1980), *Mundo mágico* and *Papaloapan* (1982) before making *Motel* (1984). After that he did *Gaby* (1987), which was in English and a co-production, and basically a Hollywood film. To be honest, I must say that I think that Mandoki is a hack. I'm not a fan of his work, which I find to be bland and lacking in personality and style.

ALFONSO CUARÓN: For someone like Luis, it was very difficult to make a film in Mexico because of the humiliations with the government, and difficulties with IMCINE. Luis was also one of the first ones to say, 'I want to make a film, and I'm not embarrassed about saying that this movie is going to cost this much to make, and so it's going to have to make this much to recoup the money.' He was a survivalist in that sense. And then when he did it, and was very successful with *Gaby*, he found the comfort in Hollywood after the spurning and humiliation in Mexico.

An English-language drama, Gaby: A True Story *tells the tale of Gaby Brimer (Rachel Chagall), a physically handicapped woman whose desire to succeed as a student causes her to triumph against adversity. Invariably and favourably compared to* My Left Foot *(1989), the film also features Liv Ullmann and Robert Loggia.*

MARTÍN SALINAS *screenwriter*: Luis and I had been living just a few blocks away from each other for couple of years in Mexico City, but we didn't meet until I attended the Havana Film Festival. Luis and a Mexican producer called Abraham Cherem and Luciana Cabarga, who was the godmother of that project, were looking for a screenwriter for Luis's project based on Gaby Brimer's real story. Luis had already worked on several attempts to adapt Gaby's life and was obsessed with the project. There was very little money, but a lot of enthusiasm. And there was the real Gaby Brimer, who had written hundreds of pages about herself and her tremendous struggle against her extreme physical limitations. I refused to read previous treatments and drafts of that project and just read what Gaby had written about herself. And what made me want to write the script was to try and tell a story about someone who struggles against her own limitations, tries to surpass them, crashes against those ones she definitely cannot, and can continue moving forward and getting involved in new challenges only when she accepts those limitations and learns to live with them. Which is how I feel about my own life . . .

I then got locked away in a house with an amazing view in Cuernavaca. Luis and Abraham would bring me the mail and the food and their notes – the perfect scenario in which to write. It took me six months to get to a serious first draft. I almost got divorced for that. But when we finished that first reading, we all knew that we did have a film there. Luis got it translated into English by Michael James Love, who came up with a few notes, which I obviously hated at first. Then we came to terms and we finally ended up writing the final version of *Gaby: A True Story* together. The script was translated in order to test the waters all over the world regarding possible producers and European actors to play Gaby's parents. I always thought I was going to get it made in Spanish, but the producers who were interested spoke only English. *Gaby* took Luis and us to the Hollywood arena from one day to another. Alfonso Cuarón had been the first assistant director. From there on, Michael and I became writing partners for almost ten years in Hollywood's 'development hell'. But that's another story . . .

*Meanwhile the 1980s also saw further fruits from the establishment of vocational film education in Mexico. Founded in 1963 and 1976 respectively, the Centro Universitario de Estudios Cinematográficos (*CUEC*)* and the *Centro de Capacitación Cinematográfica (*CCC*) collectively and individually represented the fulfilment of a much cherished dream of Mexican cineastes since the silent-film era. As the testimonies below attest, the value and function of the two schools cannot be overstated. They provided artistic lifeblood for the industry even during some of its darkest hours. The schools can claim credit for the existence of almost every single Mexican director, editor, cinematography and actor to have emerged in recent decades.*

ROSA BOSCH *producer*: Almost all of the key writers, cinematographers, production designers and directors have come out of CCC or CUEC. It's

The Centro de Capacitación Cinematográfica (CCC)

obvious that the film schools have been essential in terms of nurturing, sustaining and producing a fresh influx of talent. They have also taught people to take their talents seriously, and to approach their various disciplines as a craft.

JOSÉ LUIS GARCÍA AGRAZ: I started to work for a left-wing magazine, at the same time as deciding to study economics so that I could 'serve my country once the forces of the proletariat and the *campesinos* had seized power' (*sic*). But things don't always turn out how you expect: I found I didn't like economics and my brother Carlos, who is a year younger than me and who'd had a vocation for cinema from a very early age, encouraged me to go to the only film school there was at that time in Mexico, the CUEC at the National Autonomous University of Mexico, to study film-making so that I could do the photography on his films. The CUEC turned out to be a place where I had wonderful teachers, with whom I'm still friends, such as the great Polish-born theatre director Ludwik Margules, Alfredo Joskowicz, and the director José Estrada, who is no longer with us. It was there I discovered some of the enormous artistic and expressive possibilities that cinema offers, and my love of film-making.

In a country where the film-production sector comes second to the cinema chains and to the distributors, the film schools have the difficult task of being centres of technical and artistic learning, as well as that of resisting the globalizing intentions of governments which for over twenty years have been pursuing the demise of Mexican producers with the too obvious question: 'Why make films here when so many are already being made in Hollywood?'

The film schools – for all their limitations – have become production companies for shorts; where young people have the complete freedom to make the films they choose – a freedom that, as we well know, brings with it many other political and philosophical demands. However, it's almost impossible to create a national film sector on the basis of film schools. Budgets are very small, relations with the outside world are weak, and nor do film schools represent the totality of a country's artistic expression. What they are, though, is a breeding ground for young film-makers. Unfortunately, later faced with so many obstacles and a lack of opportunities to develop their artistic expression, many of these young film-makers go on to work in the world of television – which in Mexico is profoundly stupid – or advertising.

JUAN CARLOS RULFO: In itself, I don't think that film school teaches you how to go about things. It's you, in a particular context – all the people you meet or don't meet, all your fears and frustrations – that's what pushes you to look for projects. It was at film school that I decided I wanted to become a director; although before that I had wanted to write and, years earlier, I had wanted to be a photographer. Maybe film school was the place where it all came together and allowed me to understand what I wanted to do. But it had to happen then, it couldn't have been earlier.

MARTÍN SALINAS: I first graduated and worked as an architect in Argentina. My first step into film-making was by making animated films with an independent group of film-makers. Argentina was then suffering the most cruel and bloody military dictatorship in our country ever, so we ended up having to leave and go to Mexico. The solidarity of people like Bertha Navarro, Jorge Sánchez, Alfredo Joskowicz and many, many other Mexican film-makers and friends made it possible for us to continue with our projects as a group (Grupo Cine Sur). I wrote and co-directed several animated independent short films in Mexico and Nicaragua. But as I moved forward, I felt more and more that – at least to me – drawings were not enough; that there were many things about human beings, and their nature, that I wanted to explore, for which real human performers were needed. So I applied and was admitted to the CCC to study screenwriting.

I have no doubt that film schools in Latin America have played a key role in what has happened with Latin American films along the last ten years or so. Especially in Mexico, Argentina and Cuba. With their ups and downs, those film schools have been the actual place where older generations of Latin American film-makers who – especially in Mexico – had managed to reach the highest standards with their films in the late 1960s, early and mid–1970s, were able to pass the torch and the craft to the following generations. In countries in which the film industry as such practically does not exist, in countries where the distribution business is completely dominated by Hollywood productions (with bullying, dumping, corruption and uneven practices), the continuity between generations is always in danger.

Again, from a less epic point of view, I tend to think there's always a teacher who makes a difference in everyone's life. In my case, the CCC was not only a great chance to meet some wonderful teachers, but also a sort of point of departure to get my first jobs as a screenwriter. But if I have to mention a teacher, Ludwik Margules, who taught Dramatic Literature, was probably the one who really led me into a new level of understanding of what drama was about. Screenwriter Tomás Perez Turrent, who had written several very powerful scripts for Felipe Cazals and had been around Luis Buñuel, was also a bridge between that older generation and mine. Film school to me was not only about just learning the technical aspects of the craft, but about all the other things that no manual can teach.

HUGO RODRÍGUEZ: The CCC was my entry into cinema. Before that, I'd done some animation and lit a few shorts. But at CCC I decided I wanted to become a director, even though I graduated as a cinematographer. Film school was a place rich in ideas and in friendships. I remember my teacher, the Mexican documentary-maker Eduardo Maldonado, who taught me the importance of fully immersing yourself in a project. He used to say, 'When you're completely absorbed in what you're doing, things will happen in front of the camera almost without you realizing it.' And for that to happen, you need to be rigorous. Again, he said, 'Rigour is not the same as effort. You can spend weeks working non-stop, but if you don't put the will in the right place, it's a waste of time.'

My generation of graduates, friends and colleagues with whom I developed my vocation for the cinema, today is bearing fruit: Carlos Carrera, Ignacio Ortiz, Francisco Athié, Alfonso Cuarón, Luis Estrada, Salvador Aguirre and others.

EMMANUEL LUBEZKI *cinematographer*: I wanted to be a stills photographer from a very early age, and the two options in Mexico were the art school or the film school. I decided to go to the film school and after one week I realized that I was hooked on film and was going to shoot cinema.

The biggest influence was my not liking Mexican films, and I couldn't begin to understand why. I thought that something was wrong with me but, as far as I was concerned, they really didn't *look* good. There was something in the tone of most of the movies, in terms of acting or the fact that in most cases the sound was awful that just made them very hard to watch. There was the so-called 'Golden Era', which I personally feel is a little overrated. However, one can be more forgiving there, because it was a long time ago. What really bothered me were the movies from the 1970s. There wasn't really an industry, but there were films being made. They were mainly tiny, low-budget movies and in these films the women were invariably all prostitutes and the men were inevitably macho. These films were so horrendously lit. In fact, the acting, the themes, everything was horrible. And I didn't really love what the Mexican Film Institute was doing, which was favouring intellectual directors.

In film school we realized that we were never going to be able to shoot film, as all the films being made at this time were mainly to satisfy a demand for Spanish-language cinema in certain communities in America. Our idea was to start our own company while we were in film school and make a little money by also making a film for this market. So one night we went to a coffee shop and wrote the worse script ever. We decided to shoot *Camino largo a Tijuana* (1991) on video and sell it and use the money we made from it to shoot the kind of movie we really wanted to make. I ended up producing the film and convincing Luis Estrada, a film-school colleague, to become the director. Because his father was a famous director before him, he had a pool of actors and people who became interested in helping us. So suddenly this little tiny movie grew into something bigger.

Estrada's film was indeed respectfully received and marked Emmanuel Lubezki's feature-producing debut in 1991. It was not as a producer but as a director of photography, however, that he poised to begin a sensational professional ascent.

2

Another 'New Mexican Cinema': 1989–94

After years of drought, the early 1990s witnessed the feature-film debuts of several directors who would thereafter become international names. A new generation was on the brink of making itself heard, and these directors were conscious that something of a break from the past would be necessary if they were to assert their own identities.

GUILLERMO DEL TORO *director*: If you look at the films of the 1970s, some Mexican directors were actually very successful: [Arturo] Ripstein, [Felipe] Cazals. In their time, movies like *Canoa* or *El castillo de la pureza* were very commercial. Now the times have changed, and the audiences have changed. Many technical aspects have also changed. But many movies in Mexico remained shipwrecked in the 1970s, for almost twenty years. In those twenty years the style of photography, the style of sound design and the style of story-telling completely changed, except in this little time-capsule that is the Mexican film industry, and specifically the Mexican 'art film'. All of a sudden things changed abruptly when our generation entered. And some people just very simply didn't like this. Others are very generous and serve as a link for the new generation – in my case, [Jaime Humberto] Hermosillo and Arturo Ripstein were both incredibly generous with me when I was starting. But some others really resented it.

Some feel that the works of Alejandro [González Iñárritu], Alfonso [Cuarón] and I are among the early modern films in Mexico – they felt that finally, in film terms, we were approaching the twenty-first century. And I just feel that there are a lot of people in the Mexican industry who lived their heyday in the 1970s and wished that this decade were still all the rage. Unfortunately it's not, and, for better and for worse, time moves on. These people resent what we do. They qualify our work as being superficial or polished in an inconsequential way.

I can remember exactly the moment this happened. It happened with *Como agua para chocolate* and it happened with *Sólo con tu pareja*, and it was to do with the fact that these films were making money. I remember that a director – who shall have to remain unnamed – said to me, 'Money doesn't matter. Movies should never concern themselves with making money.' I said, 'You are absolutely right from an artistic point of view. But what you don't realize is that you are killing the industry.'

Film is an art *and* an industry. Unfortunately film is also one of the few arts that require millions of dollars to be made. A painter may require only a few hundred dollars for a canvas and some paint, but a film-maker requires a couple of million dollars. The director who said this obviously didn't realize that he was on something of an ego-trip and had forgotten one of his main responsibilities is to maintain the industry. Many cinemas like France, Italy and other European counties make perfectly valid artistic films with an eye towards the box office.

Two key directors made feature debuts in 1991. The first of these, twenty-eight-year-old Carlos Carrera, had been animating since childhood, and was still in his teens when he directed the live-action documentary short Un vestidito blanco como la leche nido *(1989). He studied at the* CCC, *and in 1991 made* La mujer de Benjamín *(*Benjamin's Woman*). Benjamín (Lopez Rojas) an old bachelor, still living with his sister, is distracted from the childish company of his older friends when he falls for Natividad (Arcelia Ramirez), a beautiful younger woman, and after an unsuccessful campaign of love letters, he and his friends plan to abduct her in order that she can fall in love with him.*

CARLOS CARRERA *director*: I had always felt a need to tell stories with images since I was very young. I drew comic strips before even learning to write. I then started to paint and even managed to sell a few paintings, which enabled me to buy my first Super-8 camera. I then started to work on animation. I started to develop stories with Claymation and drawings around twelve or thirteen years old. I made several animation shorts before buying a Bolex 16 mm camera and then completed a number of short films. I then attended the CCC. One of my teachers there was Ludwik Margules, a very important theatre director. I worked with him as an assistant director in theatre where I learned how to deal with actors. During this time I continued to make my animation shorts and to learn many of the other aspects of film-making. You learn to shoot, edit, write. When I finished the school I had four animation shorts, two fiction shorts and a documentary about a psychiatric institution for women in Mexico titled *Un vestidito blanco como la leche nido*. In the film they talk very much about love and being lonely. At the end of film school there was a contest in which you submit a project to make your first feature film. Fortunately I won and so was able to make *La mujer de Benjamín.* I was very lucky.

HUGO RODRÍGUEZ *director: La mujer de Benjamín* was the second full-length feature made as part of the CCC's 'First Work' programme, of which I am now Executive Producer. Rather than having a teacher–student relationship, Carlos and I were – and still are – colleagues of the same generation. As one of the students with the most professional experience, I tried to lend support wherever I could. At the preparation stage, I drew up the budget, trying to fit the 'foot' into the 'shoe' of our tiny budget. During filming I worked closely with Carlos as his personal assistant, and several times had to step in as unit manager in order to help the shooting run more smoothly. I even edited the film's final sequence – the fight, the robbery and the main character's escape – all intercut – and I took charge of the post-production, which we had to bring forward in time for the Berlin Film Festival to which we had been invited.

Twenty-nine-year-old Alfonso Cuarón meanwhile came up with Sólo con tu pareja *(*Love in the Time of Hysteria*). Juan Carlos Rulfo, then twenty-six years old and soon to direct himself, assisted on the production side of Cuarón's picture just as he had for Carrera's.*

JOSÉ LUIS GARCÍA AGRAZ *director*: I've known and loved Alfonso Cuarón for twenty-three years. He's my friend, my teacher; he's like a brother. I saw his work when I was a student at the CUEC and I was lucky enough to have him as my assistant on my first full-length feature, *Nocaut*, in 1982, as well as on several subsequent features. I've seen him take his first steps in cinema, and I've been close to him and followed his career ever since. He's very intelligent and possesses a vast knowledge of cinema – which, together with a love of hard work and his clear principles, makes him one of the most powerful directors around today. That his work, so rich in filmic values, can be based on a narrative skill that is at once original, direct, agile and fresh is no coincidence. His talent and versatility as a director mean that he can make a film as beautiful as *A Little Princess*, then switch to one for a young audience like the fun, edgy *Y tu mamá también* and from there move on to the third Harry Potter film.

Written by Alfonso's brother Carlos, Sólo con tu pareja *concerns a yuppie womanizer (Giménez Cacho) who contemplates suicide when a jealous girlfriend tricks him into thinking he has Aids. Initially seeking a rapid exit from the world, Tomas falls in love with Claudia (Claudia Ramírez), a beautiful stewardess herself suicidal after learning of her lover's infidelity.*

CARLOS CUARÓN *screenwriter/director: Sólo con tu pareja* was my first collaboration with Alfonso in film. We did some things previously in television, a programme much like a Mexican version of *The Twilight Zone*. It was a very low-budget production; in fact Alfonso used to call it 'The Toilet Zone' . . .

The film also signalled the beginning of Cuarón's collaborations with two men who would become the leading directors of photography of their generation.

EMMANUEL LUBEZKI *cinematographer*: I met Alfonso a long time before film school. I used to bump into him at parties and hang around in the same slightly hippy, slightly left-wing, upper-middle-class intellectual circles. We also liked the same music and the same movies, and we used to go to a movie house where they showed the best cinema from around the world – Tarkovsky, Pasolini, Antonioni. I've never found any movie theatre like that in Los Angeles. We weren't friends yet at that time, but I would see him going in and out every week, usually with a different girl . . .

I then started to work for him after we met in film school, and we simply became a team. It's hard to explain, because it happened very naturally. We like and dislike the same things and are attracted to the same stories. We also have very similar motivations. Sometimes when we work we don't have to talk about the concept of the project, that is how in tune we are.

Rodrigo Prieto and I worked together on *Sólo con tu pareja*. I knew from the moment I met Rodrigo that he was going to be a great cinematographer, much better than myself.

RODRIGO PRIETO *cinematographer*: I was actually still at CCC when I worked on Alfonso's film. Alfonso and Emmanuel saw some of the films that I was working on, and asked me to do the second unit. I jumped at the chance as I loved their work, especially *Bandidos* (1991), which Emmanuel had shot shortly before. I did *Sólo con tu pareja* for free, and I loved the experience. What I had to do was match Lubezki's lighting and, in a way, this was easy because I really liked his approach. I was on my own with a camera assistant, begging for a lens, and was allowed to do lots of insert shots, of condoms or airplanes passing. Thankfully it was a very small second unit. Shortly after, I did my first and second features, but this experience gave me the confidence to know that I could light scenes and that they would work. If my work could be put together next to the work of Lubezki's . . . Yes, it certainly helped.

As a teenager I shot little Super-8 science-fiction and horror movies and I knew immediately that I wanted to do film, I guess in whatever capacity. I applied to the CCC and took the very extensive three-stage exams. The first time, I was not admitted on the last stage. That was pretty depressing at first, but it actually became a good thing because I started working with a stills photographer that year and that's where I started to get more and more interested in the image and in lighting and composition. When I applied again to the school the following year I knew that I was more interested in photography and so likely to follow cinematography. The first time I had applied I had thought I wanted to be a director. When I was finally admitted I had that year of experience to my advantage, that understanding of lighting. During my first year, we all directed a short movie and performed roles on the films of others. I then realized that I was much more excited by being a cameraman on the shorts that I had shot than I was about the film that I'd directed. That was the moment I realized that this was what I wanted to do.

At that time I was specifically interested in the work of Néstor Almendros, Sven Nykvist, Jeff Cronenweth, and Vittorio Storaro. They all had very different styles. Almendros and Nykvist are very subtle and realistic while Storaro and Cronenweth are much more stylized. I was interested in both ways and so tried to find a method by which I could get a little bit of all of them in what I was doing. I had a lot of chance to practise among my group of twelve fellow students, as I was the only one who wanted to be a cinematographer. In my first year I shot six shorts and in my second year another six or seven. Another director did later decide to become a cinematographer but in the beginning I was the only one and so I got to shoot a lot.

It's hard to explain, but in cultures such as Mexico things are very visual and dramatic. This sticks to you in a way. With my generation there was also a friendly sense of competition. We were all checking out what the other was doing and hoping to do at least as well as the other or perhaps even better. There was a sense of camaraderie and competition really egging us on. This was certainly true in my case as I looked up to these people, some of whom had started slightly before me. For example, I was a camera assistant to Carlos Marcovich on a couple of episodes of a television series called *Hora narcada*. This series, which was mainly horror tales and very similar to *The Twilight Zone*, stopped when I was about to start shooting some of them but I did at least get to be a camera assistant. It was fun and exciting and this was the way many of us started. I think Guillermo del Toro directed some episodes, as did Alfonso Cuarón.

ALFONSO CUARÓN *director*: In Mexico until the late 1980s everything was controlled by the unions, so if you wanted to be a cinematographer you had to go through all the scales of the union and they wouldn't admit new cinematographers, it became a closed shop. The younger cinematographers were all doing commercials because it was the only work they could get that was connected to the film industry. I personally feel, though I believe in the concept of a union, that in Mexico the unions nearly destroyed the film industry. What Emmanuel and I were doing was a big reaction to that, and to the ugly-looking films that were being produced as a result.

The production designer of Sólo con tu pareja *was German-born Brigitte Broch, who had found her way to Mexico and studied dance and theatre before meeting Luis Mandoki and accepting work as a production manager on* Los Mazatecos *(1980), his documentary about an Indian tribe in Vera Cruz. The pull of theatre remained strong, but she eventually found her* métier.

BRIGITTE BROCH *production designer*: In 1987 I was offered the job of doing the art direction for *Los caminos de Graham Greene*, a docudrama for Mexican Television. That was a revelation; I loved it and never stopped doing it. To be honest, I was highly inexperienced at the time of *Sólo*, so the design was much more a result of the teamwork between Alfonso, El Chivo [Lubezki], costume designer María Estela Fernández and myself. In our discussions, our imaginations flew high. We just played with the gag, though I was also reticent to over-satirize. And visually it just built up and boomed.

Actually, *Sólo con tu pareja* had very little distribution in Mexico, the copy was pretty bad and Alfonso went to the US with it and, as you know, started an incredible career.

GAEL GARCÍA BERNAL *actor*: It was great to see a film like *Sólo con tu pareja* coming from *anywhere* in Latin America. You'd see films that left you unsatisfied, as films do, and keep on doing. And what Mexican ones there were didn't make the grade – they tried so hard to be American films that they ended up not even looking like films at all. But *Sólo con tu pareja* portrayed a reality that wasn't necessarily portrayed in films coming out of the United States. It also had a very subtle sense of humour. If I had to name one person at this point about whom I said, 'Yeah, I want to work with him', it would have to be Alfonso Cuarón.

Alfonso Arau's Como agua para chocolate *(*Like Water for Chocolate, *1992) was a watershed moment for more recent Mexican cinema, particularly on an international level. It was adapted from the novel by Laura Esquivel, Arau's wife at the time, and told of the sorrows and joys of a young woman called Tita who loses her sweetheart in marriage to her older sister, since their mother insists it is the duty of the younger daughter to be homebound. But Tita's magical culinary skills help her to save the day.*

First published in 1989, the book was a massive bestseller in Mexico (it also remained on the New York Times *bestseller list for over a year) and went on to be translated into twenty-nine languages. For his film adaptation Arau hired Emmanuel Lubezki as cinematographer.*

EMMANUEL LUBEZKI: At the time, I honestly had no real idea how to photograph a movie. I just had this instinct that told me what I *didn't* like. With *Como agua para chocolate* I tried to do a movie that I myself could watch, but I didn't have the tools or, to be frank, the craft. People obviously talk about the movie in connection with the Mexican strand of magical realism, but I think that's because of the theme of the film and the original novel, as opposed to my cinematography. Of course, the theme and characters of the film were viewed as exotic and embraced all over the world, especially in Europe. It's completely stylized and presents a very unrealistic view of Mexico. You can call it magical if you want – but people certainly loved it outside of Mexico.

LEONARDO GARCÍA TSAO *critic/academic*: I think that *Como agua para chocolate* is absolutely regressive in its representations. It's a Mexican film for tourists, one that presents a backwards notion of Mexico populated by revolutionaries and women cooking. I really hate the film. There are merits to be found in the original novel by Laura Esquivel – that offered quite a witty notion of someone falling in love with somebody who cooks. Unfortunately this became the entire basis for the film. The cinematography by Emmanuel Lubezki is also good but, that aside, this film offers a very conservative view of Mexico and the fact that it was so successful was much to my chagrin. People would come up to me at international festivals and when I would tell them that I was from Mexico that would tell me how much they loved *Como agua para chocolate* in an attempt to break the ice. It had the exact opposite effect . . .

Nevertheless Arau's film was the most commercially successful Mexican production of the 1990s and the highest-grossing foreign-language release of 1993 in the United States. It also won eighteen international awards.

EMMANUEL LUBEZKI: *Como agua para chocolate* certainly opened doors for me, at least the combination of that movie and Alfonso's *Sólo con tu pareja*. These two movies were the ones that meant that I almost immediately had agents and directors calling me from Los Angeles asking if I wanted to work there.

In terms of proximity, Mexico is close to the United States; and besides, American directors have always been attracted to cinematographers from other countries.

It was exciting. I always liked English and American movies. And I think I speak not only for myself but also for the people who I was in film school with when I say that this is what we *all* wanted to do. We loved Martin Scorsese and Francis Ford Coppola without knowing that not all American movies necessarily corresponded to this level of quality. We didn't know that there were a whole bunch of other crappy movies and that the industry was very hard. I simply had a fantasy that I was going to the land where Coppola was directing movies . . .

* * *

BERTHA NAVARRO *producer*: Guillermo [del Toro] says he deals with monsters because there is a monster part present in his own character, and he would rather it emerge in his films than in his life. I must say, I've never seen this monstrous aspect to his personality. He's the most good-natured guy I have ever met. He does have his obsessions, and I think a director *should* have obsessions. I think in the end that good directors are to an extent always making the same film.

GUILLERMO DEL TORO: Most people may remember an altered version of their childhood, but for me my childhood was the most brutal and frightening period of my life. I think that children react very naturally to horror, perhaps in a more natural and pure way to adults, and are very much exposed to it. Horror comes from the unknown and you react with horror only to things that you don't know.

Why is horror so popular? It's a morbid fascination that is part of human nature; we still secrete this fascination. It's not in *everyone*, but certainly within most people. I think that there's a thrill in seeing the worst possible outcome of anything: there's certainly a reassurance to our wellbeing to be able to witness vicariously the misfortune of someone else. It makes us, I believe, more human, to be in contact with our darker side. And it's a fact that there was a time when early civilizations believed that the world was created and destroyed every day and every night. This is how strong our fear of the dark is. The other power of the genre is that there is no other that generates images that stay embedded in your mind so strongly. For example, there are millions of people in the world who still won't go in the water because of *Jaws* or pick up a hitchhiker because of *The Texas Chainsaw Massacre*.

I used to stay up late without my parents' permission to watch *The Outer Limits*. I remember my brother and I were watching an episode called *The Mutant*; I got very scared by the make-up Warren Oates was wearing in this episode and I went to my crib really scared. My older brother put two plastic fried eggs over his face and my mother's stockings over his headband, and crept into my room. I was so scared. After that, I started waking up at night and I'd see monsters all around my room. The patterns in the shaggy 1960s carpet became, for me, a waving ocean of green fingers. I'd get so scared that I would need to pee but I was too scared to go the toilet so I ended up peeing in my bed. Of course I was punished for this, so I finally said to the monsters that if they allowed me to go to the toilet in the night then I would become their friend. Since this time, I've had a very intimate relationship to creatures.

I'd also say that, being in Mexico, I was exposed to a lot of very brutal images and situations. I saw my first corpse at the age of four. It was a highway accident. We were coming back from Lake Chapala and a red car went zooming by us and I remember my father saying very clearly, 'They're going to *kill* themselves.' And a few miles later the same car was overturned and there was a guy crying and bleeding on the side of the road. He had a bottle of Tequila in his hand. There was another guy with his butt exposed, and no head. You could see his head two metres away, dangling in the barbed-wire fence. That, plus the very gory religious imagery we have in Mexico, combined to give me a very intimate relationship with death at a very early age.

The fact is that I have a very active imagination. I lived with my grandmother for many weeks in a row and I used to sleep in an old bedroom at the end of a long corridor, and at night I would see in a super-slow-motion manner a hand come from behind a closet and then the face of a goat. I could *see* it – it might have been in my mind but it was incredibly real to me.

I still to this day don't know how to be alone. When I met my wife, I was for the first time in my life able to sleep in peace. Before that I was an insomniac. But since she has been with me, it's been twenty years of peaceful sleeping. It still takes only for me to be alone for my imagination to go into overdrive.

In terms of movies, I actually started to get excited by horror-movie stars. I wasn't conscious of the director, but of the type of movie they were. My three favourite actors as a child were Boris Karloff, Vincent Price and Peter Cushing. I would look for them in movies, because I didn't know anything about directors. I would just seek out the movies that they were in, as I knew that this guaranteed me being in for some horror.

JOSÉ LUIS GARCÍA AGRAZ: I've known Guillermo del Toro since his early beginnings; I know his short films, and I'm amazed by his narrative instinct and the passion he has for 'gore' and the horror genre. He, like Alfonso Cuarón, has become someone I'm continually learning from – I have him to thank for bringing me up to date with the world of comics. Years ago del Toro wrote a book about the cinema of Alfred Hitchcock which showed not only his deep knowledge of the art of cinema but also contained a vein of humour which has never left him – hence his ability to make horror films in which the timing and the technical perfection could be the work of any one of the great masters of the past, such as Hitch himself. Del Toro is one of those artists who is born 'already knowing': all that such artists require in order to produce work that is brilliant and full of invention are time and resources.

Del Toro took writing classes with Jaime Humberto Hermosillo but then really began his career in special effects and make-up.

GUILLERMO DEL TORO: Doing my short Super-8 films in Guadalajara I didn't have anybody to do effects for me. In fact, I didn't have anybody to do *anything* for me. I was doing the catering, the lighting, the post-sound – just everything. Little by little other people began to ask me to do the effects for their movies. I was involved in a motorcycle accident with my wife that put me in bed for several weeks. I decided then to try to learn the craft professionally in order to gain a little bit of an edge for myself and start preparing for *Cronos*. *Cronos* took me eight years to do and one of the first obstacles that I found when talking to producers was being asked, 'Well, who's going to do the effects for this movie?' When I replied, 'Me!', they expressed their lack of confidence in my being able to do this level of effects yet. I applied to a course run by Dick Smith[1] and during my bedridden days I proceeded to do

[1] One of cinema's foremost make-up and effects artists. See *Little Big Man* (1970), *The Godfather* (1972), *The Exorcist* (1973). He won an Academy Award for his work on *Amadeus* (1984).

a series of pencil and pen sketches and some very crude make-up effects. Dick Smith told me that he liked my draughtsmanship but not the sculpting or the appliances. He thought that his course would help me make my movie and so agreed to let me try it. I literally got the course and then got a job at the same time.

You met with Dick in New York and then you had to practise in Guadalajara. Then you had to meet again for an evaluation after a few months. Anyway, I would meet with producers and agree to do the job for *x* amount of money which was always just barely enough to pay for the materials and barely enough to re-invest in buying a little more equipment and materials. Eventually, when *Cronos* started, my special effects company – Necropia – had twenty people, offices and the whole thing was run as a great enterprise but we closed it at the start of *Cronos* because it had served its purpose. To this day, Necropia is a name that I own because I like it; it's my childhood.

I had written *The Devil's Backbone* with the intention of having this script as my thesis for Humberto Hermosillo. But Hermosillo was very strict on presentation, and he didn't like the way the script was formatted. He took it and threw it in the garbage, telling me that he will not read it until I learn to present my stuff more cleanly. Back in those days only the very rich writers had word-processors, and I had typed my screenplay on my IBM electric typewriter. I was so angry and so disappointed that I thought, 'Screw it, I'm going to write something else rather than go back and rewrite the same script just because the *margins* weren't right . . .' Looking back, it was not such a big loss because *The Devil's Backbone* evolved into a better movie.

Anyway, I told Hermosillo that I was going to write a story in which a young girl gives her grandfather a vampire as a pet. The very first thing that generated the idea was a paragraph in a treatise about vampires, where they say that in Europe the vampire first comes to a house and vampirizes the family, then goes out to the world. My first impulse, which is not there so much in the movie, was to make a critique of the Mexican family in which the father figure returns and sucks them all dry. I started writing this version but found it too dogmatic, as if the thesis was overwhelming both the genre and the feeling of the movie. So I thought, 'What if I make it a kind of love story between the granddaughter and the grandfather, and very much a story of acceptance?' At that moment my grandmother was dying very slowly, and I had come to accept and love her despite all our differences and the Catholic fears she had instilled in me as a child. *Cronos* is actually dedicated to her. I started to use the movie quite literally to heal – and I do think that movies can have a cathartic effect.

The absence of the father was clearer in the screenplay. The movie was about thirty minutes longer, and in these minutes the origin of the missing parents is explained. That segment was really interesting.

Cronos *begins with the legend of a Spanish alchemist who invented a small elegant device in the shape of a mechanized scarab beetle, capable of sinking its golden claws into a man and injecting a substance that bestows immortality, and a vampire's craving for blood. Centuries later, this 'Cronos Device' falls into the hands of old antiques dealer Jesús Gris (Federico Luppi), who suffers its bite. But the device is coveted by ailing industrialist Dieter de la Guardia (Claudio Brook), who sets his violent American nephew Angel (Ron Perlman) on its tail. And meanwhile, Gris's new-found urges endanger his own beloved granddaughter, Aurora (Tamara Shanath).*

GUILLERMO DEL TORO: I was doing storyboards for an action sequence in a Mexican movie called *Morir en el golfo* (1990) and Guillermo Navarro was the director of photography. Guillermo was famous in Mexico for being ill-tempered, and when I arrived on the set everybody told me that he was in a really bad mood and I shouldn't provoke him. Well, I am famous for being imprudent, so I stood next to the camera and suggested that he change the lens for this shot. He was looking through the eye-piece but stopped to turn to me and said, 'Listen, kid, do you even have any fucking idea what the lens is looking at?' I got immediately red-faced and said, 'I'll show you what this fucking lens is looking at', and walked right in front of it. Guillermo smiled and said, 'I like you.' From that moment on we have rarely had a bad day . . .

Guillermo also led me to my long-time producer, his sister Bertha Navarro. He suggested that Bertha produce *Cronos*. We met and she hired me to do indigenous make-up and effects for *Cabeza de Vaca* (1991). I said, 'How much work is it?' and she said, 'On the very worst of days you will be making up anything up to two hundred extras.' I said, 'Can I hire an assistant?'

After originally studying music Nicolás Echevarría founded the composers group Quanta in 1970. He began his career in film with a number of short documentaries, and continued to make documentary films throughout the 1970s and 1980s – frequently working on video – with his work often bearing witness to the cultural, religious and artistic experiences of indigenous Mexicans.

Cabeza de Vaca *was among the most important Mexican films to emerge*

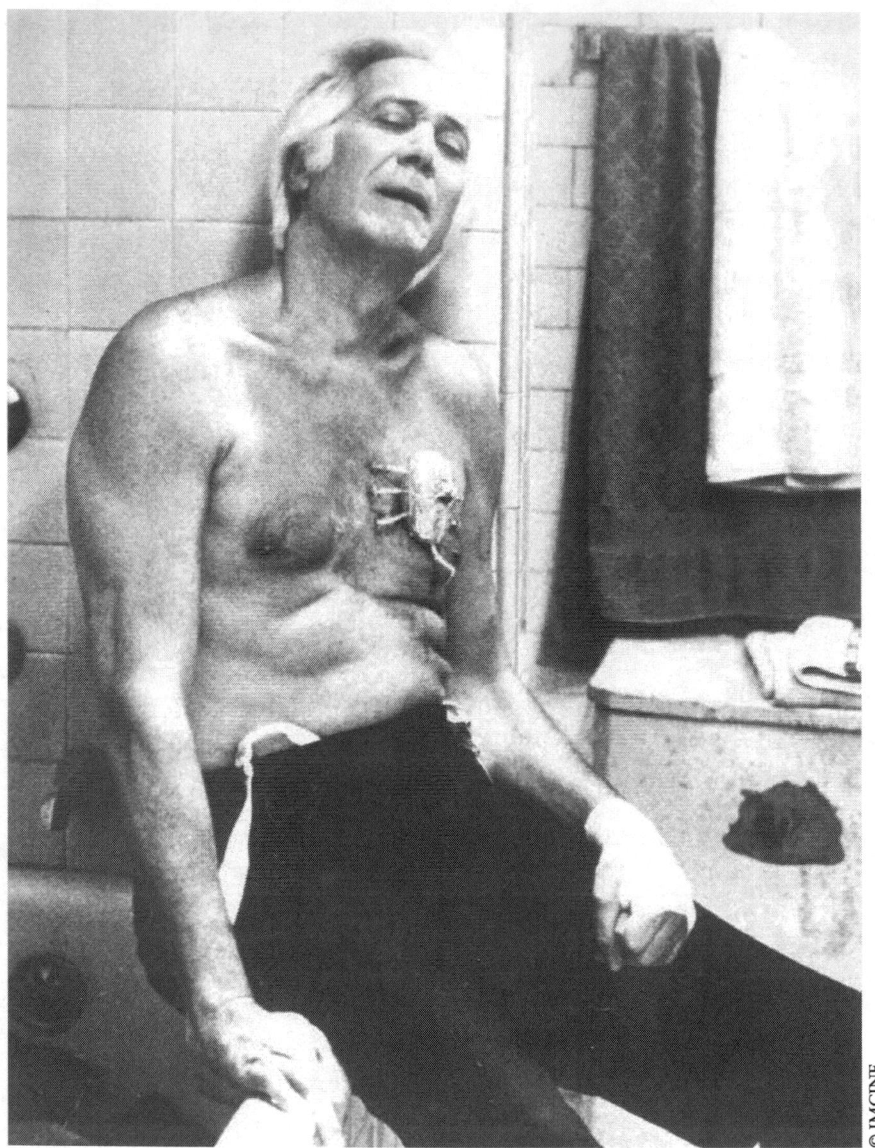
© IMCINE

Federico Luppi searches for eternal youth in *Cronos*

in the 1990s. Set during the early days of the Conquest, the film is based on the writings of Alvar Núnez Cebeza da Vaca (played by Juan Diego), a treasurer on Pánfilo Narváez's shipwrecked expedition to Florida. Combining ethnography and autobiography, the film offers a fascinating portrayal of Spanish–American conflict while also offering an appreciation of the mystical reality of native peoples.

BERTHA NAVARRO: I thought that Echevarría's vision of the new world in *Cabeza de Vaca* was so amazing and gave us an opportunity to touch upon the subject of the Conquest. It took a huge effort to make this film at the time. Again, Nicolás had this passion for the story and to touch that moment of our history was special. So much of the imagery of this film is iconic, especially the image of the cross at the end of the film.

GUILLERMO DEL TORO: I did the entire movie – a huge enterprise – with one assistant, and my wife. Bertha recognized how crazy I was in terms of commitment and loved that and offered to read my screenplay.

BERTHA NAVARRO: My brother recommended I read del Toro's script, and so I asked him to bring it to me. He was quite shy. I read the script and thought it was so different from anything happening in Mexican cinema. It was in a world of its own and, to me, quite magical. Del Toro is not just horror and gore; he has real tenderness, depth and humour. I immediately decided to do his first film.

GUILLERMO DEL TORO: Just as I say Guillermo is a brother, I feel that Bertha is one of those mothers that you also find along the way. I really love Bertha and I will never forget that Bertha believed in me, a twenty-something kid from Guadalajara who wanted to make this massive vampire project.

Guillermo Navarro and I trust each other implicitly. I only second-guessed him once, very early on during *Cronos*. He said, 'OK, I am going to do it the way you want it and then we'll see it on the dailies.' We saw his way and then my way and his way was infinitely better. We both have no ego problems and understand that collaboration is collaboration and so we are free to suggest things to each other. To this day, he understands that I am not territorial but that I do my compositions and my planning of camera moves so far in advance that if you bring another idea it has to be a very well-thought one. In terms of light I can tell him what I want only in terms of how much darkness and how much light and then leave the execution entirely to him. I really trust Guillermo completely.

Cronos is the perfect example of the feeling that your first movie will also be your last. You try to put everything that you have ever wanted to say about a particular subject in it. I wanted to show the vampiric relationship between the nephew and the uncle, and, of course, the vampiric relationship between Mexico and the United States. This is why the date in the movie –

which we see on a newspaper – is 1997, even though the film was made in 1993. I wanted it to be set in a post-NAFTA Mexico.[2]

Ultimately I think that it was very accurate in terms of what happened. That is why all the signs that you see in the street are in Chinese, English and Russian. I made a fictional Mexico that was much more cosmopolitan.

To me, the movie also explores on numerous levels the relationship that characters have with time and age and death. You have the grandmother who refuses to age by trying to fit into the same dress that fitted her last year; you have the millionaire who does nothing but shit and piss all day, living like a recluse in his room like Howard Hughes but wanting to live together just out of sheer greed. And you have the nephew who wants to change his flesh to become more handsome. The only truly mortal character in the film is the daughter, who does not care about time and is immune to the concept of death. By the same token, I wanted to show a vampiric chain that went all the way to the insect locked within the device. That's the ultimate vampire and the ultimate victim. It is locked there like a living filter and is at the same time the master and the slave.

BRIGITTE BROCH: *Cronos* was a wonderful experience, because del Toro knew exactly what he wanted. He's not only a director but also a special-effects expert and make-up artist. He created the ingenious Cronos device, and the original archangel statue.

GUILLERMO DEL TORO: The outside of the device was designed with a painter friend of mine. We sat down together and I explained that I wanted it to be like a Fabergé egg. This is obviously pertinent, because the egg is the symbol of immortality and of eternity. We filled the film with such images – for example, the serpent that bites its own tail, which in early cultures symbolized immortality. The very shape of the device was intended to remind of a scarab, also a symbol of eternity.

There was a time when the producers refused to pay for the construction of the device, and I said, 'But we absolutely need it! It's the focal point of the movie. If you don't have the inside, then you don't have the movie.' I sold my own van and personally paid for the construction of the interior of the device, which I designed completely. It was intended to look like a big factory. Microscopic drama has always intrigued me and as a child I would lie on my belly on the patio and watch ants for hours. This entomological fascination goes all the way to the inside of the device, as I wanted to have the point of view of the insect. The insect is based on a prehistoric tick. It

[2] See p. 39.

Cronos: Claudio Brook

was very elegantly designed. I sculpted the tail and my father-in-law mechanized the tail and all the interior pieces. Incidentally, most of the mechanical parts that you see were wind-up devices extracted from toys. It took us over a year to build the devices. We built thirteen of them and every single one of them got stolen at the end of the shoot. I actually like this fact – someone at some point may have opened the case full of these devices and mistaken them for the real thing . . .

Cronos *also meditates on the ancient history of Mexico with the device originally being brought to Mexico by an exiled alchemist.*

GUILLERMO DEL TORO: I was actually more interested in opening the movie like a Hollywood movie. Open it as if you are about to see a super-expensive production but then this production lasts only three minutes. Then you go in to meet the most boring guy on earth. This is what I was attracted to. It's like beginning with a Mexican version of *The War of the Worlds* with all of the spaceships arriving and then cutting to a Mexican family working in their fields on their cows and seeing the invasion from their perspective. It's really about the everyday-guy perspective of a Hollywood premise.

The image that better represents *Cronos* for me is that of the guy licking the blood from the nosebleed on the toilet floor. There were so many walkouts during this scene. What a waste; it was an extremely beautiful bathroom. There is, however, something about this shot that gets to the very root of revulsion.

Another iconic moment is the police discovery of the body being bled in the alchemist's apartment.

GUILLERMO DEL TORO: I also wanted this scene to comment on the rather sad nature of the alchemist's life. During the hundreds of years that he lived, he became a recluse – his only company was a hanging corpse. I do think that the hanging-corpse shot in particular is influenced by Hammer, and the sense that you sometimes got from their Dracula movies that it can be very lonely to be immortal.

I wish on *Cronos* that I had had a little more experience and a little more budget, and then some of the stuff would have had more clarity. That said, I am very happy with some of the images in the film, and that one is certainly one of them.

I really hate it when Hollywood shows Mexicans or Latin Americans as sweaty villains with a big moustache. I wanted to do that to the American characters. I was very conscious that they should be like comic-book villains. Ron Perlman was exactly right to bring a bit of colour and a little bit of a flourish to his character. I told him that his character was a big guy, but his nose was his Achilles heel. If you observe the movie carefully, you see him constantly smelling everything and paying attention to his nose. It's with great pride that I say that Jean-Pierre Jeunet and Marc Caro cast Ron in *The City of Lost Children* after seeing him in *Cronos* while they were jurors at a film festival.

I should point out that like most of my films, and this is something that I will do again and again, I did not set *Cronos* in any real world, I don't try to represent reality exactly as it is. I always try to take it a couple of notches above. The Spanish Civil War in *The Devil's Backbone* looks like a Sergio Leone western, except at night where it looks like a Mario Bava[3] movie. The New York in *Mimic* doesn't bear any resemblance to the real New York. Except maybe for the cockroach problem.

The production design and use of location marked del Toro's work out immediately.

BERTHA NAVARRO: We were in many ways very lucky with the team on *Cronos* but in other ways one of the real skills of producing is getting the very best people for that director. This is especially important for a first-time director – you nourish them by surrounding them with the very best people. Tolita Figuero and Brigitte Broch did the production design. *Cronos* was mainly filmed in an astonishing house in Condesa, central Mexico City. It was like a set for us, because we had the whole house to ourselves. Many of the other locations were also shot in this house – the crematorium sequence, for example. We also had a remarkable derelict factory in the south of the Mexico City [where the industrialist resides], which has since been pulled down and made into a shopping mall.

GUILLERMO DEL TORO: When I was finishing *Cronos* I was really desperate, because the first cut was horrible. I showed it to Alfonso Cuarón and he asked if I had edited the first part. I told him that another editor had done it, and he recommended that I do it myself. We tried it right there, and took out a lot of hot air in a single afternoon. He literally changed the movie.

So when Alfonso was starting *Harry Potter* [in 2003] and asked me if I

[3] Italian director/cinematographer of sumptuously styled films such as *La maschera del demonio* (1960), *I tre volti della paura* (1963) and *Sei donna per l'assassino* (1964) who inspired a wave of Gothic Italian horror films, later known as *giallos*.

would recommend some creature designers. I recommended a few that he then proceeded to use . . .

I was never the darling of Mexican cinema. The story of *Cronos* and the Mexican institutions is not a very happy one. When I first presented the film to IMCINE, they complained that it wasn't an art movie, it was a vampire film, and that I should go and get some private money. I disagreed, I said it *was* an art film and horror can also be art. They invited me to go away and storyboard the movie and come back. I did that, then they said that they wanted to see the device in a drawing. After the drawing, they wanted to see it physically, because they wanted proof that I could create it. In the end it took us almost three years to get the financing secured from IMCINE.

When we showed them the finished film, they said, 'This is a horror movie and it's not going to go to any festivals, it isn't going to win any prizes.' They felt that nobody was ever going to see the movie and that they had wasted their money. Our entire budget for *Cronos* in Cannes was ten posters and a roll of Scotch tape. All the producers, my wife and myself slept in a one-bedroom apartment. I thought that IMCINE's attitude would change after *Cronos* won twenty-five international awards and after it became one of the most celebrated films from Mexico in many years. It didn't change.

Cronos*'s impressive haul of over nineteen international awards includes eight Ariels (including Best Direction); a Silver Raven award at the 1994 Brussels International Festival of Fantasy Film; a* DICINE *award at Guadalajara; a Mercedes-Benz award at Cannes 1994 and the Audience Jury award at the 1994 Fantasporto.*

BERTHA NAVARRO: *Cronos* went to Cannes and screened in the Critics' Week, and we had fantastic press. This gave us international distribution. In Spain it became a cult film and played in theatres for more than a year. It did well in England too. In Mexico, it had the worst distribution possible. The state had sold everything and we didn't have the small theatres so we had to open in competition with a huge Hollywood star-driven picture in huge theatres. That was a catastrophe. But the critical reaction was very positive. I was slightly amazed by this, because I thought that some critics might perceive the film as not dealing with issues specifically relating to Mexico. I actually think that there is something *very* Mexican about the film and about Guillermo's films in general. There is always very strong religious imagery that relates to the fact that he had a very strict Catholic grandmother, and he equates many of these terrifying images to his childhood.

LEONARDO GARCÍA TSAO: I think that *Cronos* really adds something to the vampire genre. I also think that with this film del Toro demonstrated that he has a unique vision and that he is also able to change the rules subtly. In some ways the picture has proved to be quite prophetic . . . The film takes place in Mexico but it is a given that everybody speaks English in a normal way.

BERTHA NAVARRO: I also feel that *Cronos* was very much a film for film-makers. I remember James Cameron seeing the film in Los Angeles and being really impressed by it. What *Cronos* did obviously do was to trigger del Toro's career. It also became apparent that his imagination and special effects required more financing than Mexico could provide. In Mexico it is virtually impossible to make films that cost over $2 million. *Cronos* made it clear, even to del Toro, that he needed another structure to bring his visions to the screen.

* * *

*In a bid to reduce the public debt and encourage private investment, President Carlos Salinas de Gortari pushed through the North American Free Trade Area (*NAFTA*) in September 1993, creating a free market between Canada, the* US *and Mexico. Intended to allow the Mexican economy to expand to the extent that it could enter the 'first world', in actuality* NAFTA *led to the exploitation of Mexico's cheap labour and US companies out-sourcing certain polluting industries.*

ALFREDO JOSKOWICZ *film-maker/Director,* IMCINE: The *sexenio* of Carlos Salinas de Gortari [1988–94] had been a disastrous period, during which many of the state production companies were terminated. Conversely, private production continued to flourish. At this time, there were around fifteen private companies and all of their films were distributed by Películas Nacionales. The films were exhibited on Compañía Operadora de Teatros (COTSA), the state-owned exhibition circuit, which was very advantageous tax-wise for the private producers. However, in 1991, for different reasons and for various motives, this arrangement was terminated and in 1993 the state sold COTSA. It was an important moment of this period under President Salinas that in 1993 Mexico entered NAFTA.

BERTHA NAVARRO: The landscape really changed after NAFTA was signed. Before NAFTA, we were able to produce a decent number of films annually. Quality-wise, the films were a mixture of the good, the bad and the ugly, but we *were* able to produce them. After NAFTA we produced, I believe, just eight films. It had a massive impact on the industry. Prior to NAFTA it was largely state production – something with which I have never been involved – but after NAFTA it was completely the opposite, a totally open market, with nothing in between and no period of transition. Now we have different rules to the game.

GUILLERMO DEL TORO: I remember at the time that I felt that NAFTA was so ill-planned, because it was passed without getting any consensus from the world of culture as to how best to protect the industry and the local culture. We were raided and invaded by media companies and there was nothing there to protect us.

ALFREDO JOSKOWICZ: Prior to joining NAFTA there was a very important law – albeit one seldom respected – dictating that Mexican cinemas had to show a certain minimum percentage of locally produced films. In the first three years of joining NAFTA, this percentage was reduced to 30 per cent, then to 20 per cent, and then to just 10 per cent. However, NAFTA did have an important effect on exhibition in Mexico, because it allowed exhibitors to increase ticket prices. With this came the proliferation of the American-style – and frequently American-owned – multiplex screens that did bring much improved screening facilities and improved technical specifications.

You also have to take into account the new freedom of choice Mexican audiences faced. Previously the cinema would have two, maybe three screens. Now they had eight. Of course, if you wanted to see spectacular special effects and big stars then you would invariably pay to see an American film. But if you wanted to view a representation of your identity then you would choose to see the Mexican film. That is, if the film was good. If it wasn't, why would you pay to see it?

This is perhaps the beginning of a new story: because, from an industry on the point of collapse, there finally came signs of regeneration.

3
Adventures in Hollywood, and More Generational Stirrings

In 1994 Alfonso Cuarón took up his first Hollywood engagement, directing an adaptation (scripted by Richard LaGravenese) of Frances Hodgson Burnett's A Little Princess *for Warner Bros. Updating its action to the First World War, the film tells the tale of ten-year-old Sara Crewe (Liesel Matthews), raised by her father in India until he heeds the call to war, and so places Sara in a magnificent New York private school run by the stern Miss Minchin (Eleanor Bron), where Sara introduces the other girls to the joys of make-believe and makes a spirited adjustment when her circumstances suddenly and tragically become straitened. Enthusiastically greeted on release, the film was praised as a formally audacious, sensitive and humanist rites-of-passage story. It won Cuarón a New Generation Award at the 1995 Los Angeles Film Critics Awards and also saw Emmanuel Lubezki nominated for an Academy Award for his cinematography.*

JOSÉ LUIS GARCÍA AGRAZ *director*: Alfonso Cuarón and Guillermo del Toro understood that if they wanted to find fulfilment in their chosen profession, they'd need adequate resources in order have continuity and development, which is why they emigrated to Hollywood. I suppose many other film-makers have had the same idea – although not everyone possesses the 99 per cent of artistic rigour and 1 per cent of holiness that these two have.

ALFONSO CUARÓN *director*: I ended up in Hollywood not because I wanted to; I ended up in Hollywood because I didn't have any *choice*. When I did my first film I burned my bridges with the government, and I knew that if I were going to go back, the way of doing films in Mexico or the ways *I* knew of doing films in Mexico would have to change. Most films had a big percentage in terms of input from the government; my first film had 40 per cent. To survive as a film-maker in Mexico you had to sustain yourself by doing lots of work that had nothing to do with cinema – stuff like commercials. I didn't want to go from being an assistant director with Luis Mandoki to making commercials. *Sólo con tu pareja* premiered at the Toronto Film Festival and I knew I had a choice: I was completely in debt but immediately started getting offers of work from Hollywood. There was an open door and I went to pursue that open door and I'm very thankful.

I don't see Hollywood as the 'dark side'. Again, it's all about film, and in this regard the idea of working in Hollywood is irrelevant. Paul Thomas Anderson works for studios but so what? For me, independence has nothing to do with budget – and this is where many mediocre film-makers shelter themselves. There are people who do amazing masterpieces for nothing and at the same time there are people who make crappy films for nothing. My point is that Hollywood is what it is: it's an industry, and I don't feel that the mission of Hollywood is to corrupt film-makers. There are talented people working in that industry and mostly, yes, there are mediocre people who don't care about cinema but do care about power and money. But I can't classify things as simply as: 'This is a Hollywood film: it's bad. This is a Mexican film: it's good. And this is an Iranian film: so it's good. And this is a big-budget French movie: it *must* be bad . . .'

Guillermo del Toro had been having a tough time finding the means to follow up Cronos *– at least, until a Hollywood studio came calling.*

GUILLERMO DEL TORO *director*: Four years passed between *Cronos* and *Mimic*, and they passed because I didn't know then what I know now. At the end of *Cronos* I was in incredible personal debt, to the tune of a quarter of a million dollars; I may have made a career on the film, but I certainly didn't make any money. And I was desperate, because I was in no position to have that kind of debt. My father helped, he told me he would assume the debt, but that he wanted to be paid back in dollars. Then I watched in horror as the value of the dollar rose . . .

Then, out of the blue, came an offer to meet with Universal Studios to discuss the possibility of a project. They explained that they would pay me $125,000 for writing a screenplay. I was immediately interested, but I told them I would do it only if the screenplay were something I really wanted to do. And so I wrote *Spanky*, based on the novel by Christopher Fowler. I really think it's one of the best things I've ever written. Perhaps because of that, it was rejected by the studios, who said it was too dark, and unlike any other movie in that it sounded like a comedy but ended up as a tough horror film. I said, 'Exactly! That's the whole spirit.' I lost about a year on that one . . .

Then I started developing a period project, and Universal told me they didn't do period movies. Lo and behold, a few years later – *The Mummy.*

But after two years came the chance of doing *Mimic* as a short film – part of an anthology movie. At the same time I was also developing *The Devil's Backbone* but we were finding very little support in Mexico. So I was trying to do a Mexican film and I couldn't; I was trying to do an American film and I couldn't. When I pitched the *Mimic* short to Bob Weinstein at Miramax's Dimension outfit, he loved the story and said, 'Why not make it into a feature?' I must say, my first response was, 'It's a perfect short but is there enough here for a feature?' But it had been three years since I'd made a film, so I said yes to it. I learned a lot after that . . .

Mimic *proposes a classic horror plot. After a disease carried by the common cockroach has reached epidemic proportions in Manhattan, entomologist Dr Susan Tyler (Mira Sorvino) genetically engineers a mutant species of insect that can exterminate the roaches before dying out itself. The venture is a seeming success but a handful of years later Susan learns that people are disappearing and corpses turning up in and around the Manhattan subway. The mutant species has proved more durable and adaptable than she intended and so alongside her colleague and partner Peter Mann (Jeremy Northam) and reluctant New York subway cop Leonard (Charles S. Dutton) Susan sets out to destroy the mutant race she has unwittingly unleashed. Ostensibly a subterranean sci-fi thriller,* Mimic *is also a convincing allegory about genetic manipulation and, a recurring del Toro preoccupation, how the ghosts from the past come back to haunt us.*

GUILLERMO DEL TORO: *Mimic* remains the hardest shooting experience of my life – it's still right up there, pricking at my pain threshold. There were many reasons. Back then, it was the most expensive movie Dimension had made and also by far the most expensive movie I'd ever done. I experienced many hardships with it. I sustain the belief that you learn through pain, and I certainly learned a hell of a lot. One of the main things I learned, and which I cherish to this day, is that you are *always* making two movies. You are making the movie that the screenplay is telling, and you are making a movie that is pure image, pure cinema. Cinema has a kinship to theatre and other forms of drama in that it needs a narrative, characters and an arc, but in fact a film may also remain full of memorable images in spite of the screenplay not being completely there, or screwed with by the powers-that-be. And that is the most intimate part of the movie and the part that nobody should be able to take away from you. That was a revelation, almost like an out-of-body experience. To this day I can see this being the case with film-makers such as Dario Argento and Lucio Fulci. Sometimes their films can be completely incoherent but out of this mass of incoherence a beautiful and absolutely powerful image arises.

As well as being hard for me, it was also a hard movie for Miramax to make and I didn't make it any easier on them. At the end of the day, with a cold head and a cool heart, I see that they wanted to do *Alien* and I wanted to do *Mimic*, and so we ended up with *Alien 3-and-a-half* . . .

American films seldom show child characters coming to harm, but Mimic *surprises us in a scene where a child who breaks into a basement is first terrorized and then mercilessly killed.*

GUILLERMO DEL TORO: Horror is an extension of the fairy tale and in fairy tales ogres and wolves eat children and I think that it goes to the roots of story-telling to have children as vulnerable. It's something I really take very seriously when I make movies. To me it's more dangerous to show kids in a movie about giant dinosaurs, and pretend like the dinosaurs won't eat them. In reality, they would. I think it's best to show that, should a child ever encounter danger, then he or she should act cautiously. Children don't necessarily need to fear what they know – such as the granddaughter in *Cronos*. But they do need to show caution towards that which they don't know. If they don't, just like adults, they are apt to pay the consequences.

I shot that basement scene very slowly over a single day, paying very careful attention to pull back and show the final moments from a wide angle. That was for fear of censorship. With every frame I shot, I feared that it would never be included in the final movie. Thankfully it is, and it remains not only my favourite scene from the film but I think among the very best things I have done. I don't like *Mimic* as a whole, but that scene, and the scene of Mira Sorvino being abducted on a subway platform, are two of the best scenes I have ever shot.

There was some stuff shot by the second unit that I detest. I refuse to shoot fake scares, and *Mimic* has a couple of them. One is the girl leaving the building with her bicycle; that sequence is absolutely ridiculous. The other is of the boys finding a derelict under a plastic bag. I really hate 'jump' scares. I can safely say to this day that I have never shot one of those. There are also things on the first unit that weren't done by me, and I really find them very defective. They lessen the movie. I still love the moments I mentioned, and I still love the stuff in the abandoned subway. Actually, the scene where Charles S. Dutton's character meets his death was a sequence that they wanted to give to the second unit and Charles and I stood united and said,

'Screw that.' I love that death. It's an unexceptionally beautiful death that we took a great pride in shooting.

One of the ways in which del Toro responded to his troubles on Mimic *was in the formation of the production company Tequila Gang, in which he was joined by Laura Esquivel, Bertha Navarro, Rosa Bosch and Alejandra Moreno Toscano.*

BERTHA NAVARRO *producer*: All Guillermo's Spanish-language films and projects are done through Tequila Gang. Guillermo also wants to help other people so that they can have the same break that he did, and this is another function of Tequila Gang.

Spanish-born Rosa Bosch moved to Los Angeles and began working at Filmex, the American Film Institute Film Festival in LA. In the early 1980s she attended the Havana Film Festival, a force that brought all of Latin America together in large numbers.

ROSA BOSCH *producer*: When I went to Havana I discovered that there was an incredible heritage of Latin American film-making that I knew very little about. It gripped me in a very passionate way, a little like falling in love. In Havana I not only met some great people but was privileged enough to watch a lot of films that are very difficult to access, particularly films of the third cinema, the ground-breaking political cinema from the 1960s which was a major force at the Festival and in the international arena. Then I began to go back even further, exploring the Brazilian cinema of the 1940s, the silent cinema of Mexico and Argentina, the Mexican cinema of the 1940s, the so-called 'Golden Era'.

The whole boom has always been celebrated as a Spanish–Latin American thing but the attitude of the Spaniards until recently was always very condescending. At that time in Havana there were actually very few Spaniards running around. Then came the celebration of five hundred years since the discovery of Latin America, and out of that came quite a change in attitude.

I was then appointed Deputy Director of the National Film Theatre in London and of the London Film Festival. Sheila Whitaker, the Director at the time, was extremely interested in Latin American cinema. I was given a fantastic opportunity to do a huge number of seasons focusing on national cinemas from Brazil, Mexico, Argentina and Central America. At the end of my time in London I took something of a semi-sabbatical but remained on the Committee of the San Sebastián Film Festival. It was around this time, while on a trip to Mexico, that Bertha Navarro mentioned to me that she and Guillermo del Toro were thinking of setting up a production company. This was Tequila Gang. Bertha was the driving force and we went into it full force and full of enthusiasm, even though we had no backing for the venture. It was a very good mix of personalities. Bertha and Guillermo were already very close. Bertha, of course, is historically a very important figure in Mexican cinema. Having me on board to look after some of the business aspects of the company and the launching of the projects just seemed to make perfect sense.

Because we all have to eat, we also started handling films from other people and other production companies. This increased on a greater scale after I worked with Wim Wenders on *Buena Vista Social Club* (1999), which provided a key link into Cuban cinema and Cuban culture.

From the beginning we presented ourselves as people who understood the business, and wanted to *do* business. We also helped unite film-makers in a desire to be seen, and to be commercial. Unlike the film-makers of the 1960s, most of whom were driven by a purely artistic or political force but despised the business side of the industry, Guillermo del Toro, Alfonso Cuarón and Alejandro González Iñárritu, the guys we have emerged alongside, all understand the business side of film-making. Instead of sitting around and bitching – 'We're on the other side of the world and nobody's interested in the films we're making' – they have really gone out and shaken up film-making and grabbed the interest of the world. It's similar to what later happened with the Argentinian group. They want to be in the world and for their films and culture to be visible. What brought about the change, I think, was primarily their analyses of and frustrations at what had come before. All of these film-makers are very ciné-literate, highly educated and very savvy both technically and artistically. In a business sense they are all very confident and competent.

This is the driving force; the desire to have a place in the market. They are also aware that as a film-maker you really have artistic freedom and space only if you also have box-office success. One often generates the other. Freedom is not given to you; it has to be earned. They have also watched the previous generation of film-makers grow quite bitter and angry and have made a resolution that this is not going to happen to them.

The film-makers were of a new generation, with an age range of late twenties to early forties. Of this generation I think that Cuarón is the oldest but he is still relatively young. *Como agua para chocloate* was directed by an older director; Alfonso Arau is now in his mid-sixties. There is a big difference. Arau also came out of a very different milieu. The newer generation of directors we are talking about are well travelled, very cosmopolitan and emerged in a very different cultural moment in time.

* * *

After completing the short films Un muy cortometraje *(1988),* Malayerba nunca muerde *(1988) and* Amada *(1990) Carlos Carrera – who began making short animations aged only twelve – attended the Centro de Capacitación Cinematográfica (*CCC*), studying under important theatre director Ludwik Margules. Carrera's first feature, the multi-Ariel-nominated* La mujer de Benjamín *(*Benjamin's Woman*) (1991) was followed by the comedy-crime hybrid* La Vida conyugal *(1993). This was a project beset by financial difficulties and Carrera put the experience behind him with his third feature,* Un Embrujo *(1997).The film is set on the Yucatán peninsula in 1928. Eliseo (Daniel Acuña) is the son of a violent stevedore, and faring poorly at school. But his teacher Felipa (Blanca Guerra) takes an interest in him and, though she is in love with a sailor, winds up having a sexual encounter with the boy, which inevitably stirs up gossip and trouble, not to say local superstition.*

BERTHA NAVARRO: Carrera had done those two films prior to *Un Embrujo* and, quite simply, I liked him very much. I was also impressed by his animation work. What's very clear is that the film I made with Carlos was his most personal. He has covered other subjects and worked from other scripts that were given to him, but I think that even above his first film, *Un Embrujo* is the one that meant the most to him. I liked the fact that Carlos had a passion for the project, felt that it was a story that had to be told. As a producer I need that passion from the director – I don't believe in compromises. In Mexico we have so few film-making opportunities that when we do make them we should always try to make jewels. There's no room for mediocrity.

CARLOS CARRERA *director*: It took us about ten years to make *Un Embrujo* and it was originally supposed to be my second film. It is based on a book by a good friend, Marcel Sisniega, who had written down the stories as told to him by a very old man. I found the material fascinating and very original. It was also very Mexican. It happened in a region that has very seldom been portrayed on film. We also placed the story in a period that had not been shown on film before, a very interesting time in Mexico's history. When I started working with Bertha Navarro I also met Martín Salinas.

MARTÍN SALINAS *screenwriter*: After several years of mostly 'development hell' and writing in English, with no directors attached to the projects in most cases, or not meeting with them at all along the whole development process, teaming up with Carlos Carrera and Bertha Navarro for *Un Embrujo* was a blessing. Not only did I have a director to talk to, but one whose favourite drama teacher at CCC was the same as mine. What he had on paper were a series of wonderful, powerful moments in the life of a man who Marcel Sisniega had interviewed over several months, written as a series of vignettes. The story started in Yucatán around 1923, and spanned several years, with no dramatic structure at all. He had been trying to turn these pearls into a screenplay and needed someone to build a story with what he had. He told me he didn't want the story to concentrate on just a childhood story, but to try to give the feeling of a life going by, to span several years of Eliseo's life – from childhood to adulthood but with a clear dramatic unity. I agreed because that was the kind of thing you felt when you read all of those fragments. The other thing that we wanted to keep and strengthen was this amazing cultural mix of conservative Catholicism, Marxism and Mayan pre-Columbian cultural background that prevailed in Yucatán in those days – sometimes even within the same character.

We first talked for days about the characters and what the father–son aspects in those fragments suggested to us. Then we worked together on a first tentative structure. I then flew back to Argentina – where I had returned to live – and worked on my own until I was able to send Carlos a first storyline and outline. He liked it and we continued working until we got to what we felt was the main storyline: the story of the son of this idealist union fighter at the docks who deals with frustration by drinking too much, a mischievous kid who has this dream of living a very different life to the one his father lived, and doesn't want to follow in his steps. The romance with his teacher is a possible way for him to find this way out of that world. But it is obviously an impossible dream and as he grows up he can't help finding himself in his father's place and has to cope with this until he is pushed by circumstances to take some decisions as an adult. We all have been involved in a father–son story in our lives. I felt I knew what I was writing about and that we had a very clear common denominator with Carlos on that, without needing to say a word about own father–son personal stories. Once we had this storyline clear, we travelled to Yucatán on a research trip and found lots of very original stuff and events in the newspapers of those days and stories told by the older people in Puerto Progreso, to build the plot.

RODRIGO PRIETO *cinematographer*: Originally *La mujer de Benjamín* was going to be Carlos's thesis project at CCC and I was going to work on it, but Carlos had the opportunity to turn it into a feature and I couldn't work on it because I had not yet finished my studies. You wouldn't *believe* how disappointed I was. That said, Xavier Pérez Grobet did a truly wonderful job on it. I had always wanted to work with Carlos and so we began to discuss another movie that also sadly never happened. Then, at last *Un Embrujo*. The film was very different from anything I had done before, and Carlos was worried that I was into only very stylized and sleek movies when in fact I just thought that this style was what was best suited to some of these movies. Carlos wanted something much more subdued and realistic and I was also very eager to also explore this avenue. *Un Embrujo* was the perfect opportunity to do it. The style of the film is very simple and I really enjoyed working with a naturalistic type of lighting. Carlos is also very visual: he draws incredible storyboards but he is not stuck on the visual side as his emphasis is on the drama, the narrative and the characters. He was very good to work with. He let me do my thing while also encouraging me to try doing less.

On the evidence of Un Embrujo *it was obviously very important to Carrera that he relate stories and places that connect specifically to Mexico and Mexican history. From an early stage he was viewed as one of the leading voices in contemporary Mexican cinema.*

CARLOS CARRERA: I didn't, and still don't, pay much attention to that. I want only to make the films and to tell the stories I like – that is, stories about common people in common situations. I really don't care too much about such things; I also don't pay any attention to box-office results. It's the stories I believe in. I feel comfortable with the stories I know. I am not a nationalist but I like the stories that I know better.

* * *

FRANCISCO GONZÁLEZ COMPEÁN *producer*: You know, everyone talks about 'New Mexican Cinema' and many see *Amores Perros* at the forefront of this boom, but for me it all started with an earlier film that was not as successful as *Amores Perros* – Salvador Carrasco's *La Otra conquista* (*The Other Conquest*). It was very well marketed by Twentieth Century-Fox and it opened well on what was for Mexico a large number of screens.

Carrasco's film takes place one year after Hernán Cortés's arrival in Mexico, and opens with the infamous massacre of the Aztecs at the Great Temple. The lone Aztec survivor of the massacre is a young Indian scribe, Topiltzin (Damián Delgado), illegitimate son of Montezuma. Spanish friar Diego

© Andrea Sanderson

The American poster for *The Other Conquest*

(José Carlos Rodríguez) has been charged with converting the native 'savages' into civilized Christians, but naturally finds Topiltzin to be a tough assignment.

SALVADOR CARRASCO *director*: My sisters had a lot to do with my passion for cinema. As a teenager they would take me to art houses in Mexico to see films that marked me for ever. Then it became a ritual for me to go on my own. My approach to some of these films was almost religious, treating them as cultural icons that transcended everyday existence and made me feel, think and learn things I hadn't experienced before. Intimate films with universal dimensions. Some personal favourites that always come to mind are Lelouch's *Les Misérables* (1995), Saura's *Cría cuervos* (1976), Wenders's *Wings of Desire* (1987), Teshigahara's *Woman of the Dunes* (1964), Scola's *Le Bal* (1982), Kieslowski's *The Double Life of Veronique* (1991), Tarkovsky's *Nostalgia* (1983), Kurosawa's *Ran* (1985), Claire Denis's *Chocolat* (1988) and Buñuel's *Los olvidados* (1950).

My producer Alvaro Domingo and I met in the first week of college and immediately we hit it off. Although we come from different worlds, we share many artistic objectives, and thus complement each other very well. *The Other Conquest* is a quintessentially independent film in that, in order to do it our way, we took seven years to make it, from 1992 to 1999. As an exemplary producer, Alvaro carried it through from beginning to end. His faith in the project was unfaltering, and there is no question that this film would never have happened without his commitment, perseverance, loyalty, hard work and, ultimately, an unconditional respect for the integrity of my vision as the writer–director of this film.

The first seed, so to speak, came to life on 13 August 1991. I remember the date so distinctly because it was the four hundred and seventieth anniversary of the fall of Mexico-Tenochtitlan, I was in New York, thinking about my country's origins – the sort of thing one does more often when abroad. And I felt like reading something about that historic day, which is how I came upon Vasconcelos's *Brief History of Mexico*.

One of Mexico's leading philanthropists and businessmen, Manuel Arango, had generously granted me a scholarship to attend college, and after my graduation from New York University, we discussed the possibility of making a short film about the Conquest for the Expo '92 in Seville. In October 1991, I presented him a treatment of the film, which was then called *The Absolved Vision*. Fortunately he liked it very much, and that is how the seed money came about. Then over some *tacos de cochinita pibil* in a restaurant in Coyoacán, I suggested to Alvaro, with whom I had made a couple of short films at NYU, that we join forces, he as producer and I as writer–director, to make this short film together. He read the treatment, fell in love with it, and we resolved to create our own company, Carrasco & Domingo Films, as a framework to take the big plunge together.

It wasn't long before Alvaro and I saw in the story the potential to turn it into a feature film. Neither he nor I then knew exactly what we were getting into, so our primary motivational drive has always remained to tell Topiltzin's story as best as we could. We both believed there's something in this story about resistance and preserving one's identity and beliefs that would be appealing to different kinds of people, just as he and I were originally drawn to it for different reasons.

So I worked on the feature screenplay. Alvaro showed it to his father, Plácido Domingo, who was able to read it on a plane from Europe to New York, and was very moved by it. Needless to say, Mr Domingo himself embodies the best possible form of syncretism between Spain and Mexico. Once he agreed to participate as a co-producer, the fundraising odyssey had officially begun. Mr Domingo also sings the aria 'Mater aeterna', composed by Samuel Zyman originally for the film, in the end credits. Another significant co-producer who later came into the project was Enrique González Torres SJ, who is currently the Dean of the Iberoamerican University in Mexico. Mr González's faith in the film has been a continuous source of inspiration for us. He believes that, bottom line, *The Other Conquest* helps remind everyone that Indians are an intrinsic part of Mexican history and contemporary society. At the time of the film's narrative, the 1520s, there was an ongoing debate in the courts of Europe about whether Indians had a soul or not.

In August 1992 we decided to shoot some sequences in order to generate credibility and dispel a certain notion that this film couldn't be made. We obviously didn't have enough money to shoot the whole feature yet, so we shot as much as we could, until the money ran out, and we were not able to resume until June 1995.

I should also point out that at Bard College I took a wonderful literature course with Mary McCarthy, with whom I developed a friendly relationship. Among other things, she was kind enough to bring a collection of poems of mine to the attention of Octavio Paz and Carlos Fuentes. One day she urged me to read a short story she believed would affect me profoundly: Vsevolod Garshin's *The Scarlet Flower*, about a man who in the most adverse of circumstances – such as being confined in a mental asylum – becomes obsessed with the idea of stealing a flower that embodies all evil; thus he would redeem mankind. The premise resonated deeply within me, perhaps because of its Don Quixote-like connotations, but also because it embodies a simple truth: life makes more sense if you have something to fight for.

In fact, that story couldn't be further away from the subject-matter of *The Other Conquest*, but an interesting turn of fate happened. A few months later, I was reading a book my father gave me, the aforementioned *Brief History of Mexico*, and it occurred to me that at the time of the Spanish

Conquest of Mexico, an Indian who had been deprived of everything might have tried to conquer, so as to possess and absorb, the powers of a statue of the Virgin Mary – in whose name questionable things were being done – in order to redeem himself and his people. The twist was that 'to conquer' would not imply destruction, but to regain his own Aztec Mother Goddess through the Virgin Mary, the utmost symbol of the invaders. In Topiltzin's and in Friar Diego's minds, the Virgin Mary and the Mother Goddess become one and the same. Ultimately, I think the film is a parable about cultural tolerance.

The main thing was to tell that particular story in a context that had always fascinated me for its complexities and ambiguities, its poetry and its harsh brutality. Just to imagine those encounters, the misperceptions – Moctezuma believing Cortés was the God Quetzalcoatl; the friars believing conversion could happen overnight; the mere idea of 'conquering', the will to resist expressed in mysterious ways, the religious fervour, the other-worldly sounds . . . anywhere you turn you find movie material. I'm just surprised there aren't many more films out there about the Conquest. One of the most significant contributions of our film has been to heighten interest in a topic so vast and complex that it deserves to be treated with a multiplicity of voices, stories, and points of view.

We raised the money mostly through private investors and rather symbolic contributions from Mexican institutions that support the arts and culture. There were hundreds of phone calls, letters, and appointments throughout the years. It was a painstaking process, with many ups and downs, countless disappointments and a few occasional breakthroughs that made it possible in the end. I am in complete awe of Alvaro as a producer for pulling this through, for not only was the subject-matter and scope of the project regarded with scepticism by many people, but he was also trusting a first-time, ambitious, completely unknown twenty-four-year-old writer–director.

Damián Delgado was undoubtedly the best casting for Topiltzin. At the time he was dancing in a brilliant company called Ballet Teatro del Espacio. He was a first-time actor. Subsequently, he was one of the leads in John Sayles's *Men with Guns*, among others. I was looking through the video camera during Damián's casting session, and when he said the line 'Hicieron cenizas de mi pueblo; ahí quedó hecha humo nuestra verdad de las cosas . . .' ('You turned my people into ashes; our truth went up in smoke . . .'), it became very clear to me that he was not acting, as he knew what those words meant. He was Topiltzin. Incidentally, during the shoot people never called him by his real name.

We had a first-time writer–director and editor, first-time producer, first-time lead actor, first-time production designer, first-time composer. But our art director was Brigitte Broch, who went on to win an Oscar for her superb work in Baz Luhrmann's *Moulin Rouge*.

BRIGITTE BROCH *production designer*: I read of the period through books and novels set during this era to help me get the feel of mood and time. I tried to use colour not only from an aesthetic point of view but also in connection with its symbolism and relation to the state of mind of the characters and their spiritual voyage. I prepared a Zapata project for Alfonso Arau – a film that fell through then – but had the great fortune to work briefly on two occasions with Vittorio Storaro. His colour theories have embedded themselves in me and I try to be aware, to use colours with utmost care as to their significance. So, *The Other Conquest* was really no more difficult than any of the other movies I have worked on. It involved research, locations that don't betray the period and detail to the spaces in order to make them believable.

SALVADOR CARRASCO: I went to every possible archaeological site within a three-hundred-kilometre radius surrounding Mexico City, where the production was based. I was looking for an intimate setting far away from the metropolis, where clandestine rituals would still be taking place without the Spaniards immediately realizing ... though of course, eventually they would, like in the film. What we see in the film is not, and did not ever attempt to be, the great Mexico-Tenochtitlan that Bernal Díaz del Castillo described. It is a post-Conquest look, since the present time of the film begins in 1526, five years after the fall of Mexico-Tenochtitlan.

Other sets include sixteenth-century monasteries, underground caves, colonial plazas, etc., which one still finds in Mexico. Of course we had to make up and retouch them for authenticity. Slight architectural licence was taken for the sake of spectacle, but we always remained true to an internal aesthetic coherence.

In terms of location permits, the real breakthrough took place when Alvaro pitched the film to the Director of the National Anthropology and History Institute, who told Alvaro that she had always envisioned a serious, committed, Kurosawa-like approach to this subject, and that here was the opportunity to fulfil that.

The logistical challenges could be summed up in an unforgettable phrase that my first assistant director once told me: 'The problem with you, Salvador, is that you're trying to make a first-world film with third-world resources.' I am convinced that the biggest asset of this film was that most of the people who worked in it genuinely believed they were doing something worthwhile, something about a subject we all carried in our veins and yet were regrettably ignorant about, since many of the issues raised by the film are still taboo in Mexico. And yet, the film had an incredibly positive response in Mexico, becoming the highest-grossing Mexican film ever when it opened in 1999.

The opening sequence at the aftermath of the Great Temple Massacre was filmed in the archaeological site of Tenayuca, which is situated in the heart of Mexico City. The camera placements had to be carefully chosen, for moving the camera an inch in any direction would have revealed the local market, buses, phone cables, etc. The rain hoses weren't powerful enough, so we had to spend many hours fixing them versus a few hours shooting one of the main events in Mexican history! That was my first day of professional 35 mm shooting ever. But I was hooked.

The shot of the Spaniards discovering the clandestine ritual was filmed in 1992. The reversal of the Indians reacting to their arrival was shot three years later. Thanks to our ingenious production designer, you don't notice the difference. In the process, actors aged, even disappeared, and the sacrificed princess was now dripping milk from breast feeding, which was a beautiful metaphor for the idea of rebirth through sacrifice.

The title has three levels. First it refers to the religious or spiritual conquest that followed the military conquest of Mexico; second, to the Conquest of Mexico focused on an 'other', an indigenous protagonist – the Aztec scribe Topiltzin, illegitimate son of the Emperor Moctezuma; and third to the 'conquest' carried out by the indigenous peoples themselves, who appropriated European religious forms, and made them their own. The Virgin of Guadalupe, which combines the Aztec cult of the Mother Goddess with the Catholic veneration of the Virgin Mary, is perhaps the best example of this 'reverse conquest'.

My goal was to narrate a passionate story, one based on a careful imaginary reconstruction of what things might have been like during the decade between the fall of Mexico-Tenochtitlan, capital of the Aztec Empire, in 1521, and the alleged apparitions of the Virgin of Guadalupe to the Indian Juan Diego in 1531. This decade constitutes what we might call the gestation period of the contemporary Mexican nation; it is a period fraught with complexities and ambiguities which are still relevant today, five hundred years later.

Frequently, when the indigenous peoples of the time of the Conquest are portrayed, they come across as entirely passive, as if they had just simply and unquestioningly accepted the things imposed on them by the Spaniards. *The*

Other Conquest depicts a creative and critical indigenous culture which, despite all sorts of losses and setbacks, makes an effort to assume an active role in the shaping of its own destiny. The characters in the film show us that, even under the most adverse circumstances, people will strive to carry out their own 'conquests'.

In other parts of the world, the 'encounter' between European and 'native' peoples was resolved by the outright annihilation of the indigenous groups. The social consequences of the Conquest of Mexico are especially profound, in that in Mexico the indigenous peoples, through their violent and partial incorporation into the official and religious life of New Spain, managed to survive.

The new, hybrid, *mestizo* race which is Mexico was certainly not the result of a tidy and idyllic process of harmonious interaction. Still, I don't think that it's a good idea to adopt a facile Manichaean point of view, that sees history as a black-and-white story with good guys and bad guys. *The Other Conquest* explores different levels of the Spanish Conquest of Mexico, a remarkable historical process whose relevance has in no way been diminished by the passing of five centuries.

This picture is not just about Aztecs and Spaniards; the topics it explores are relevant to all ethnic or national identities that were formed in the crucible of colonization, conversion, and syncretism. *The Other Conquest* is an invitation to dialogue, an opportunity to reflect on our origins and respect our differences.

La Otra conquista *opened in Mexico on 4 April 1999. Released on twenty-seven screens, by the end of the film's first week the film had grossed $216,038 with a high screen average of $8,001. Expanding over the subsequent three weeks to a maximum of seventy-two screens, the film grossed an impressive $1,507.306. Opening in seventy-four screens in Los Angeles on 19 April, the film dominated industry headlines, grossing $400,000 on its opening weekend alone. It went on to finish among the highest-grossing foreign-language films of the year in America.*

* * *

Juan Rulfo is widely regarded as one of the greatest writers in the history of Mexican literature. An exponent of magic realism, perhaps his best known work is Pedro Páramo, *in which the book's narrator, at the behest of his dying mother, visits the deserted village haunted by the memory of his patriarchal father.*

After working on both La mujer de Benjamín *and then* Sólo con tu pareja,

Rulfo's son, Juan Carlos Rulfo, emerged as a singular film-making talent in his own right during the mid-1990s: first with El Abuelo Cheno y otras historias *(*Grandfather Cheno and Other Stories*), then with* Del olvido al no me acuerdo *(*I Forgot, I Don't Remember*).*

JUAN CARLOS RULFO *director*: *El Abuelo Cheno* came about as a result of ignorance and ingenuousness. I had wanted to tell a story that moved me deeply, but I was worried that a story personal to me would not be interesting for the spectator. Yet, at the same time, I was sure there was something in it that could justify making a film. Curiously enough, the only thing I'd done before then was a 'Making of' documentary of Carlos Carrera's first full-length film, as well as a lot of interviews with a bunch of old men. I wasn't concerned – I'm still not – by the formal and/or conceptual distinctions between fiction and documentary. *El Abuelo Cheno* represented the discovery that the personal can have value as narrative, and that you can learn from that. You could say that what I achieved in the film was achieved unwittingly, although I was learning along the way.

My father did have an influence, of course. But it was to do with discovering the process of introspection that an author has to go through in his work. Rather than being close to my father in the sense of reinterpreting his work, I think it's something more intimate and personal: a son learning from the steps and the paths taken by the father – which, in a mysterious way, have an existence very close to mine. The part of his work that I feel closest to is his photography. It's there that you see his attitude to things. The way he framed a photograph, the atmosphere, the feeling it imparts – all comes together perfectly, allowing an apprentice like me to fathom from it an approach to life that, doubtless, will be with me for ever.

When talking about *Del olvido*, it's important to bear in mind *El Abuelo Cheno*, which tells the story of the tales surrounding the death of a character called Cheno – my grandfather. Originally, however, I'd been trying to find people who had known my father, who had lived in the same region. I didn't find anything out about my father, but, on the other hand, I did discover all these real characters who led me into a fascinating world full of stories and sensations I just couldn't ignore. That's why I came up with the structure of the death of the grandfather – to provide myself with a pretext for telling all the other stories. *El Abuelo* is basically a short told in a circular structure, without taking too many risks. It was my answer to what had seemed the failure of not finding what I had been looking for: my father.

Later on I decided to keep on looking, but making use of the seeming failure of the non-meeting, basing myself on the things people had forgotten, in order to continue telling their stories. Let me add that it's these stories that attract me the most, much more so than the direct testimonies concerning my father, which, although I did get them, didn't offer as much, in filmic terms, as the other characters. *Del olvido* is a work full of loose ends, in which the themes of memory and the transitory nature of life allow me to play with very evocative atmospheres and film time. Memory and the fleeting nature of things are both very cinematographic.

It's perfectly normal for people to feel uncomfortable in front of a camera. We can take that as a given. It's really a question of not treating people as though they were material for a news report. You need a great deal of time, and they do too. If you expect to get everything on a first take, then think again. In this particular case, the working plan stated that the most important thing was to get right up close to daily life, to the pace of life there, and to listen. All the crew, cameraman and sound recordist, knew exactly when to turn on their equipment; they'd learned to sense when the words we needed were approaching.

The film was well received, although I think the results could have been much better. Critics and producers, who reckon they know about these things, want me to accept the numbers. They argue that it was enough that a documentary of such a personal nature was even able to enter the big-screen battle of midsummer 2000. Ten prints went out, compared to 250 for *The Perfect Storm*, 250 for the *Flintstones in Viva Rock Vegas*, and 250 for *Amores Perros*. It remained in cinemas for over eight weeks and for a similar length of time on video and in video shops and clubs.

All this, it should be said, was achieved despite the total scepticism of the distributor, who invested very little in promoting the film – still the case today now that a DVD version has been edited and has yet to be released. *Del olvido al no me acuerdo* remains in circulation thanks to word of mouth, which has gradually become the film's real promoter. In this sense I'd go as far as to say that it's a film that, over time, has become more powerful.

4
The Making of *Amores Perros*

In turning to the impact of what became the signature film of the New Mexican Wave, it is necessary first to consider certain trends in Mexican film exhibition during the 1990s, together with the domestic success of a 1999 picture entitled Sexo, pudor y lágrimas *(*Sex, Shame and Tears*).*

ALFONSO CUARÓN *director*: What happened is that, for many years, the Mexican people stopped going to the movie theatres, because the theatres were so lousy. First they stopped going to Mexican films, then they stopped going to films in general. Most of these films were financed and released by the government. IMCINE couldn't really have cared less; its function was political, in that they had to state that they made twenty films per year. These were films that nobody saw. Though, I must add, there are now some good people at IMCINE . . .

FRANCISCO GONZÁLEZ COMPEÁN *producer*: The cinema ticket price was controlled by the government, so there wasn't much money coming back to the producers, and the quality of the films declined to that point that people finally stopped going to see them. Then in 1995 the price controls were terminated, and bigger exhibition chains started to flourish. We not only got a lot of screens, but better quality too. These new theatres also cultivated a new audience, the more affluent classes who had previously avoided the cinema because it was such a low-grade, shabby experience.

ALFONSO CUARÓN: In the mid-1990s, there were new chains of cinemas, multiplexes. When you walked into one of these, it was no different from being in a cinema in the US, right down to the concessions stand. My memory of cinema from childhood is related to Mexican candies, now it was all Hersheys . . .

FRANCISCO GONZÁLEZ COMPEÁN: So, now we had all these lovely cinemas – but they were completely filled with American films because Mexico was not producing any films of its own.

ALFONSO CUARÓN: When the middle classes started going back, there was a film called *Sexo, pudor y lágrimas* by Antonio Serrano.

Serrano's comedy drama concerned a pair of young couples in Mexico City: Ana (Susana Zabaleta) is starved for love by her intellectual husband Carlos (Victor Huggo Martin) at the point when their friend Tomas (Demián Bichir) returns from many years of foreign travel. Over the street, promiscuous executive Miguel (Jorge Salinas) and his unhappy wife Andrea (Cecilia Suárez) are visited by old friend María (Mónica Dionne). Inevitably, the two visitors stir up the marital relations of their respective hosts.

Released on 16 August 1999 on 138 prints by Fox, Sex pudor y lágrimas *became at the time the highest-grossing locally produced film at the Mexican box office.*

ALFONSO CUARÓN: What was interesting was that it didn't open particularly big – but on its second week, when most Mexican films throw in the towel, instead of dropping it did a little better. The third week it did even better. And it just kept on escalating. People in the industry began to say that there was an audience for this film – which had proved more popular than many contemporary American films – and so they decided to distribute Mexican

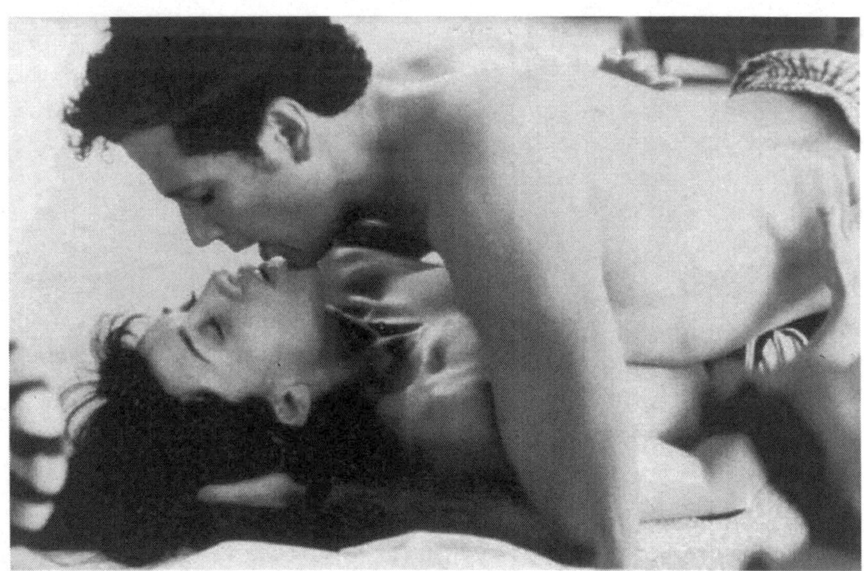

Bringing Mexican audiences back: *Sexo, pudor y lágrimas*

films again. Not enough to regenerate Mexican productions, but enough to ensure that films such as this began to be seen.

ALFREDO JOSKOWICZ *film-maker/Director,* IMCINE: In 1997 Mexico produced only nine feature films, the lowest number since 1932 so the government was compelled to help; FOPROCINE (Fondo de Fomento a la Producción Cinematográfica) was created to assist quality films.

In the last five years, we have used FOPROCINE funds to assist forty-seven films. The government put $13.5 million into FOPROCINE, a fund that was responsible for *Sexo, pudor y lágrimas*, a film that attracted an audience of 5.3 million people. *El crimen del padre Amaro*, another FOPROCINE-assisted film, also achieved in advance of 5 million viewers in Mexico and has gone on to be the most successful Mexican film in our history. Unfortunately, even with these successes, the fund is not enough, and the $13.5 million has not been recouped.

JOSÉ LUIS GARCÍA AGRAZ *director*: FOPROCINE has a committee of senior figures who can award your project, if selected – you need to submit your script, budget, plan of financing, etc. – up to $700,000. Even in Mexico a film nowadays costs around $2 million. In other words you're going to need at least as much again in order to start filming.

BERTHA NAVARRO *producer*: The release of *Sexo* marked an interesting moment, because it was one of the first big local successes in a long time and was also, I think, the first time that a major company had distributed a Mexican film. It's also a very open, fresh and sexually frank work that the young people in Mexico identified with – it was not moralistic. But it was quite a broad comedy of the kind that has been done many times in Europe, so for audiences outside of Mexico it wasn't really able to offer anything new. To all intents and purposes, it was *Amores Perros* that served notice or gave affirmation of the fact that we in Mexico can make films that compete with any made anywhere in the world.

GAEL GARCÍA BERNAL *actor*: There are four key aspects to *Amores Perros*. The first was the attention paid to the film from those people in the industry who supported it. The second was the quality of the film itself. Third was the fact that it was a big box-office hit in Mexico and claimed a place in the market. Fourth, and the basis of all this, is that it was a privately owned film. I must also tell you that the amount of work that Alejandro [Iñárritu] and the producers put in to make sure that this film was seen was *unbelievable*.

* * *

AltaVista Films, the Mexican production outlet that would nurture Amores Perros, *was originally set up as a joint venture between Corporación Interamericana de Entretenimiento (*CIE*), Latin America's leading live-entertainment provider, and investment capitalist Sinca Inbursa. The creative team at AltaVista had funds, but not so much experience: Francisco González Compeán came from advertising, while Martha Sosa was a former television journalist.*

MARTHA SOSA *producer*: Alejandro Soberón [chief executive of CIE] was the crazy visionary who said, 'Let's make a production and distribution company to do the films that we want to do.' My job at AltaVista was to look for those films and for that talent. This was also the job of Francisco González Compeán, the director general of the company.

Previously I'd had a long career as a journalist in radio and television. I also owned a very successful television production company with my husband, but I'd grown tired of this career. I'd always been a film buff, and many of my friends were film-makers. Being a film-maker then was not as it is now. It was extremely difficult, and not made easier by the fact that many film-makers simply didn't care about audiences. They would claim that they wanted their films to be widely seen, but they were often elitist in their approach. I think that this is a major difference between many of the film-makers at work today in Mexico and those who were operating in the late 1970s and 1980s.

FRANCISCO GONZÁLEZ COMPEÁN: My father is a lawyer and a politician – so there was surprise, on my part as well as my parents', that film was the career I chose. In fact, I went to business school first, but in retrospect that was a smart move because very few people at film school actually care about or understand the business side. Then I was about to enter Columbia University in New York to study Public Administration, but I began to have doubts. I'd taken some screenwriting classes at NYU and realized this was something I wanted to get further into. So, I took a Masters in Media Studies, specializing in film production. And I loved it, because whenever a teacher talked about financing or the contract details of a production, I was the only one paying attention – everybody else wanted to get their hands on a camera and get the hell out of the room. Nobody wanted to be a producer. But I came to the conclusion that's what I wanted to be.

Before going to the US I had worked in advertising, and when I returned to Mexico I had some bills to pay off so I got back into the strategic planning area of advertising. That really helped a lot in terms of finding a system for connecting with people. So, I had a business background, a little advertising background, and a little film background. And when students ask me what they need to become a producer, those are the three disciplines I recommend.

After a year or so in Mexico, Martha Sosa, Monica Lozano Serrano, Yissel Ibarra and I started toying with the idea of film production. It all came together when Alejandro Soberón, the President of CIE, who had started in film, pledged his allegiance to us, then we put together a business plan for AltaVista Films. AltaVista also spawned a sister distribution company, NuVisión, for Mexico and Latin America. At that time in Mexico, 1998, just having a business plan was a first, because everyone approached film on a single-film basis – the industry was completely devastated, there was simply no production. In the mid-1980s there would be maybe a hundred films produced per year, very low-quality, cheesy productions, but there were lots of them. And 450 million tickets would be sold a year. By 1998, ticket sales were closer to 80 million, and only four or five films were shot that year. We were at rock bottom.

At that time, you had two kinds of producers. First there were those making low-budget exploitation films, and for a number of reasons – the ticket price, the falling audiences – they were running out of gas. The second kind of producer was the art-house type who wasn't concerned with anything but getting the film made and maybe taking it to a couple of festivals. Frequently these films weren't even released in Mexico. Or if they were, they were released on very few screens. They didn't really care about the movie being seen by lots of people, in fact they *frowned* on films that were seen by lots of people and so created this very elitist little clique, because they made their money out of actually producing the film, not through selling tickets.

To have a huge bank and a huge entertainment company backing film production was shocking. When we announced the formation of AltaVista and NuVisión, we had to choose our words very wisely. We couldn't say that we wanted to make commercial films, because then we would be labelled as anti-culture. So, we came up with the statement that we wanted to make films that a lot of people would want to see. This wasn't received so badly . . . but it's absurd that we had to be so careful. Surely the aim of making a film is to make something that a lot of people are going to want to go and see?

We started to develop. We said, 'We can't pay for stars' – which, at any rate, we didn't have at this time in Mexico – 'and we can't pay for special effects. So this has to be a story-driven studio. Director-centred, and story-driven.'

The first film AltaVista made was *Todo el poder* (*Gimme the Power*,

2000). It was a comedy, and very local, but it also says some very strong things, so much so that some of the executives at the company were slightly worried by it. It directly deals with a theme very close to that of *Amores Perros*, the insecurity that comes from living in the city. It was very successful, and great fun to produce and market. It didn't do well outside of Mexico, but it was exactly the kind of film that we wanted to make.

Thanks to my marketing background, I proposed the idea of market research, and that was another first. What it revealed was that people didn't mind happy endings; they also liked romantic endings – but what they *really* wanted was to be able to recognize themselves on the screen. Film is about reality, and film constructs reality. We always called it 'the little mirror'. So we really wanted to make provocative films in which the Mexican people could recognize themselves. And the moment that people in Mexican films started to look and speak like real Mexican people, they went crazy.

* * *

BERTHA NAVARRO: González Iñárritu wasn't from the film community, and in some ways he was like del Toro – a guy who seemingly came out of the blue, but was pure talent.

ALEJANDRO GONZÁLEZ IÑÁRRITU *director*: First of all, I am an autodidact and a kid from the streets. I lived in a neighbourhood very similar to that of Octavio and Susana in *Amores Perros*. The green mosaic on the front of Octavio's house is an *hommage* to my house in the Narvarte neighbourhood.

I grew up with parents who taught me love and education as my main tools, but with three sisters and one brother it was a very, *very* limited economic situation. Because we were five I didn't get that much attention, therefore I was very free-spirited, growing up and learning about life on the streets from the time I was eight years old. At sixteen I escaped, hitchhiking, with my girlfriend, in search of myself, selling jewellery on Mexican beaches.

Twice – first at seventeen, then at nineteen – I boarded a cargo ship crossing the Atlantic: once from Vera Cruz and another time from Coatzacoalcos. On the first trip I spent three or four months. The second time, I remained in Europe, surviving for one year on a thousand dollars. I did every kind of job to survive, including picking grapes with the gypsies in Spain and dancing in a swimsuit in the pool of a discothèque. I think these two experiences taught me more than any university.

Then I returned to Mexico to create a rock band, to be a serious musician – and a film-maker, after seeing the film *Yol* (1982). I had started to study

Communications when suddenly a friend of mine, Mariana Garcia Barcena, offered me an opportunity to be a DJ, because she liked my voice. So I had a three-hour show where I could play, say and create anything that I wanted. I learned to entertain people with my favourite music, my characters and ideas, and my bizarre imagination. I then became the director of the station at twenty-two years of age, and was listened to by millions of people in the biggest city in the world.

After five years, I thought that I had completely cracked radio and considered myself a master of the medium – so I suddenly felt poor. I quit when WFM was the most important and influential radio station in the country because I realized that I wanted to make films, and communicate through a visual medium. To do this I had to learn how to work with images. I was lucky. After the huge success of the radio station, I received the opportunity and support from Miguel Aleman – my former WFM boss – to create the corporate image of a huge TV corporation. With my partner, Raul Olvera, I started to write, produce, direct, edit, post-produce and sell approximately eighty commercials a year, this for the next five years. It was crazy, but this was the first time that I went on a set as a director. My only experiences had been with a Super-8 camera when I was eleven – that, and having been the assistant director and composer for a short film taken from a story by Julio Cortazar directed by Pelayo Gutiérrez during university.

I have learned skills by doing them. I learned film on sets, doing horrible things, experiments, failing and spending more time on them than in my own house. Also important to my development was my theatre studies with Ludwik Margules, a great teacher who strengthened and expanded my concept of directing. But it was the commercials that gave me the opportunity to play with all the tools, to understand the mechanics, to create and explore in thirty or sixty seconds, different genres, tones, beats, rhythms – and, most importantly, to have a camera, a couple of actors and tell a story and say something through images and sounds. All of the things that I have directed were written and produced from the beginning to end by me so that gave me the best education in the world, the freedom and the tools to make anything happen.

The problem with the commercials was that they filled your pocket but emptied your brain and soul. It was not a wise interchange. So after five years I decided to quit, and I wrote and produced with Pelayo a thirty-minute pilot, *Behind the Money*, for TV, with Miguel Bose as the star. It was a great exercise to confirm to myself, before making a feature film, that I could direct something larger than thirty seconds. My goal was to have at least one good scene, just one would have been enough for me – and there is one scene that I still like today. With the next step, *Amores Perros*, I thought, 'Should I? Can I?' Now, today, I know that I can.

Pelayo Gutiérrez helped me produce *Behind the Money*. But I was desperate because they loved the pilot, but it was never accepted as a TV series – it was too expensive to shoot. I was developing an idea about a family from Guerrero and their two young sons who began to involve themselves in the guerrillas of Chiapas with Subcommandante Marcos and the consequences of that. And I wanted a writer to help me, so I wanted to read scripts. Pelayo sent me a very good one that was fluid and extremely well written. I said, 'Who is this guy?' It was Guillermo Arriaga.

GUILLERMO ARRIAGA *writer*: I have always been interested in writing, and I think this was because when I was about twelve years old I was very shy; I was incapable of saying to a beautiful girl, 'I like you.' So I wrote thousands and thousands of words to say it. And there is still a shyness inside of me.

I was finally able to go to a very good school called the Mexican-American School, after having been in schools from which I was expelled; I have Attention-Deficit Disorder so it was always easy for me to lose concentration and get distracted. At the Mexican-American School there was a course where we were given the opportunity to work in theatre, writing, directing and working with actors, and here I discovered Shakespeare and a lot of writers of the Spanish 'Golden Age'. At sixteen I wrote, produced and directed a play, and it transpired that the cast didn't like the ending. They said that if I didn't change the ending they wouldn't perform it. I said, 'No way.' The day before the play was due to be performed, it was cancelled. I then began writing a story for a children's supplement in a newspaper.

It was at about this time that I became seriously interested in politics, and became of the belief that revolution was much more important than writing. But I then went back to it, because I became ill and found out that I had developed an infection in my heart. The doctor treating me disclosed that he had good news and bad news: the good news was that I was not, after all, a hypochondriac; the bad news was that I risked dying because my heart was so swollen. I was told to remain in bed for three months. During this period I read Jorge Luis Borges for the first time, decided that I wanted to be a writer, and began to write short stories. Then nothing happened, I became a little bit despondent, feeling like I had no talent.

A last throw of the dice was my applying for a writing scholarship at the National Institute of Fine Arts, which I won. I subsequently wrote a novel in approximately ten days – wrote it as if possessed. I entered the novel into a writing contest, which it didn't win. Fortunately, Laura Esquivel read it, liked it and recommended it to her publisher who decided to publish me. The novel was *Relato de los esplendores y miserias del Escuadrón Guillotina y de cómo participó en la leyenda de Francisco Villa*. After this came my second novel, *A Sweet Scent of Death*; my third, *The Night's Buffalo*, and a collection of short stories, *Retorno 201*. I was approached by Gabriel Retes who had read and admired *A Sweet Scent of Death* and wanted to make it into a film. The finished film is one that I absolutely dislike. It wasn't a pleasant experience and if it were possible I would take my name off of it. At one time Alfonso Cuarón was going to do it but . . . [*pretends to cry*] he didn't.

I had written previous screenplays, *Amores Perros* was just the first to be filmed. It is really the second film in a trilogy that began with a screenplay called *Upon Open Sky*, which has yet to be filmed. I have the option to direct it. *Upon Open Sky* begins also with a car accident. I have experience of this. Once there were seven of us in a jeep returning at six in the morning from a hunting trip in the north of Mexico. The passenger in the front seat somehow distracted the driver, and we went down a deep cliff. Suddenly I was in the middle of breaking glass and twisted metal. It was especially horrifying for me because I was sleeping in the back seat when it happened. But miraculously we survived because we were carrying huge metal coolers on the roof. Then suddenly people I didn't know and wouldn't ordinarily come into contact with surrounded us . . . I became obsessed with what happens before, during and after an accident.

I was teaching at the university in Mexico City. A mutual friend heard that Alejandro had read *Upon Open Sky* and liked it and so set up a meeting between us. We went to a restaurant, where I asked him two very personal questions. I cannot reveal to you either the questions or his answers, but his responses demonstrated that he was a very interesting, complex and profound man, and somebody that I wanted to know.

ALEJANDRO GONZÁLEZ IÑÁRRITU: Guillermo has been a teacher all his life, and I had previously made some declarations about how bad my teachers were and expressed my belief that cinema could not be taught in classrooms, that cinema was outside, in real life.

GUILLERMO ARRIAGA: I of course ribbed him about being the fucking guy who had gone around telling everybody that the university was no good when there were professors there killing themselves in order to ensure that they were doing a good job . . .

ALEJANDRO GONZÁLEZ IÑÁRRITU: Guillermo was initially so mad at me, like,

'Who do you think you are?' But I think that deep down he thought I was right.

I told him that I was developing a project and I would love for him to write it. We started to work, but ten days later he called me back and said that for personal reasons he couldn't continue with it.

GUILLERMO ARRIAGA: It was basically a comedy. After more meetings and four or five attempts I had to say to him, 'Listen Alejandro, I'm not one to commit the ideas of others to paper, I can only write personal stuff.' So I suggested that he and Carlos Cuarón work together on the comedy, since Carlos is a brilliant comedy writer. After I had said goodbye, I immediately thought, 'Shit!' So I told him about the screenplay I was writing that involved three parallel stories. And I told him it was very dark. But he was adamant that he was interested.

ALEJANDRO GONZÁLEZ IÑÁRRITU: We started working together based on that idea and it all fell into place from there. As he was writing the film, I was already directing it in my mind. Sometimes I discussed the blocking of the actors that I had in my mind with Guillermo, so that he could translate that in the script. Every book, every song, every smell and everything that I absorbed over three years helped me to know and reveal the characters, and then to be able to share that with Guillermo. I participated very closely in the idea, concept and design. But it was Guillermo who wrote, solved and conceived the thing, and who I consider one of the best screenwriters in the world.

GUILLERMO ARRIAGA: Alejandro is a perfectionist and he is also very obsessive. He considers every angle of human condition. He also has a brilliant sense of humour; you should see his commercials. He is a man who has big thoughts and is not afraid to reflect on life. We have a constant dialogue throughout both the screenwriting and the film-making process. We are living proof of the myth that the writer and the director are adversaries. There is an absolute mutual respect.

* * *

GUILLERMO ARRIAGA: For me, the epitome of the human condition is contradiction. The more contradictory the character, the more human and interesting they are. I personally avoid making characters likeable; I want to make interesting characters, not likeable ones. Some of my characters are despicable but rather than the audience liking them I want them to understand and perhaps recognize them.

Mexico City is very complex, very interesting and very difficult to understand. It is a strong presence within itself, and, as the biggest city in the world, it's an anthropological experiment – there's no way it could not be a character in the script. I think that there are cities in the world that can be there or not – Mexico City has far too much power for that. I cannot escape it when I write.

I think that my major influence is perhaps the street. I want the films I write to look real; and I would hope that anyone watching *Amores Perros* would say, 'The guy who wrote this, he was *there*.'

Arriaga's screenplay for Amores Perros *was finally structured as a triptych of overlapping and intersecting narratives, exploring the lives of disparate characters who are catapulted into unforeseen dramatic situations, instigated by the seemingly inconsequential destiny of a dog named Cofi.*

GUILLERMO ARRIAGA: In terms of the structure, my Attention Disorder helped me. When I was at school it made some of my teachers think that I was mentally retarded, but this chaotic thinking actually works for me in film. Things go back and forth and stories mingle. Faulkner is without a doubt my major literary influence: *The Sound and the Fury; The Wild Palms; Absalom Absalom!* and *Light in August*.

The three male characters represent an archetype divided into three different stages: a guy under twenty; a guy in his forties and a guy in his sixties. In a certain way these represent who I am. So the film is autobiographical, absolutely.

I was the owner of the real Cofi. When I was eight years old, everyone in my neighbourhood had a dog. Cofi was an ugly dog, a mixed-breed combination of a Labrador and a Weimaraner. When I was nine I was watching television and there was a knock on the door, and I was called to be told that Cofi had killed the champion of the neighbourhood. My neighbours took my dog and they fought him against the dogs of opposing neighbourhoods; Cofi became a champion. He was so fierce that sometimes he arrived home with small dogs still in his jaws . . .

In Story No. 1, Octavio (Gael García Bernal), Cofi's teenage handler, enters the dog into brutal fighting contests, hoping to win enough money so that he can elope with Susana (Vanessa Bauche), the appealing young wife of his aggressive brother Ramiro (Marco Pérez). A near-fatal injury to Cofi prompts a reckless car chase that ends violently in a dreadful crash.

GUILLERMO ARRIAGA: The hardest and most problematic for me was the first story. Remember, this has lots of characters and mainly takes place on the outside. The second story has mainly two characters, trapped on the inside. The first was riskier for me as a writer. Then again, I like to take risks.

We can see my characters as like Adam and Eve, they are often on their own and they don't have a society that will comfort them and give them space. The only thing that sustains two lovers is love itself. There is nothing else. This is why forbidden love for me is very important.

In Story No. 2, middle-aged businessman Daniel (Alvaro Guerrero) discovers that dreams can become nightmares, after he abandons his family to set up house with a beautiful young model, Valeria (Goya Toledo), who will then be severely injured by the car crash and ultimately lose a leg.

Initially Valeria is presented as the kind of shallow media creature who appears on TV to announce to the delighted audience that she is dating a movie star, and dotes on a small dog called Richi. After Daniel installs her in a part-finished apartment, the dog disappears down a hole in the floorboards.

GUILLERMO ARRIAGA: I did want to show the stupid superficiality and the obsession with celebrity. I wanted to make a very strong point about the superficiality within the media and show how this superficiality can suddenly and very quickly lead to hell.

Daniel is really in love with Valeria and makes sacrifices for her, accepting her as she now is after the crash. I think also that sympathy for Valeria is harder won, because she's much younger than him.

I had the story of a woman with her little poodle – I hate women who use pooches in this way – but I didn't have the link until Alejandro told me the story of a woman who had lost her poodle under the floorboards.

I love dogs and think they represent the kind of person you are and so in *Amores Perros* I did want them to represent their owners but I also wanted to use them to make a wider point about the human condition. In the first story you have an innocent boy who slowly becomes a murderer, just as you have an innocent dog slowly becoming a murderer. Then you have a beautiful dog with a beautiful owner who loses everything and slips into a living hell, just as the dog is also trapped in a living hell. Finally, you have a hit man who meets his canine counterpart.

In Story No. 3, El Chivo (Emilio Echevarría), a revolutionary-turned-assassin, witnesses the accident and finds that it leads him to a life-changing moral epiphany. Not least, he also becomes the adoptive owner and guardian of Octavio's dog, Cofi.

The final shot of El Chivo heading into the horizon allows for a certain ambiguity.

GUILLERMO ARRIAGA: Many people ask me why he is leaving and I always say that he is going to review his life and come back when he is better. I wanted there to be room for optimism.

* * *

ROSA BOSCH *producer*: Remember, on paper a film such as *Amores Perros* would have frightened even many private companies. For a start, it was long, it had dog-fighting, and a very complex narrative structure. But still, it could only have been made privately. IMCINE would never have been able to finance it fully. The average cost of a film in Mexico is $1.5 million dollars. If IMCINE gives you half a million dollars, how are you going to get the rest?

GUILLERMO ARRIAGA: I must stress that I am not against state-funded cinema. I think there are some films that *have* to be state-produced, but what happened in Mexico was that suddenly the state was the *only* producer of films – so it wasn't the good film-makers who got to make films, but the ones who had the best contacts within the government. What Alejandro and I are both critical of is the friends-in-high-places scenario. I also take exception to those directors who said 'I am going to make this movie and I don't care if anyone goes to see it or not.' With the cost of one film you could build a number of schools. So I think that the film-maker does have a certain amount of responsibility. Personally, I want my work to be seen as widely as possible – England, France, Vietnam – not just Mexico. This doesn't mean that you have to be purely commercially minded and make endless concessions.

Alejandro had been very successful at everything he'd done, and was already very well known within Mexico. I also had been published. So the moment that we went out into the market AltaVista films and Martha Sosa were very keen. I want the input of Martha Sosa to be fully recognized because she was the one that pushed this film to be made.

The only problem we had was with audiences and the commercial potential of the project because, as other producers were quick to tell us, Mexican audiences were largely used to broad romantic comedies, not a brutal, urban film involving dog-fighting. Martha was not concerned only with the commercial potential of the film, she was determined to make it whether it was commercial or not.

MARTHA SOSA: I had admired Guillermo and Alejandro for a long time – Guillermo, incidentally, was also one of my professors in Communications Theory at university. During my years as a journalist I hosted a radio show dedicated to cinema – and not just Mexican cinema, because there wasn't enough of that. But I wanted to introduce to the new audiences what newer Mexican cinema was about, because there was such a prejudice at the time, the common consensus being, 'If it's a Mexican film then it must be really bad.' I started inviting directors on to the show to talk about their work, mainly younger directors who were just starting out and who had perhaps made only shorts. But I interviewed Alejandro when he made *Behind the Money*. And that show would be the only filmed piece I had on which to sell Alejandro to investors. I didn't show investors his commercials, because everybody knew that they were very good but also very expensive . . .

I felt I could bring interesting and positive aspects to the project, starting with convincing investors to become involved. But also I'm the kind of producer who does get involved on a very personal level. And that's what happened with Guillermo and Alejandro – I knew immediately on reading the script that there was something very powerful dragging me into it.

I wasn't sure at that moment exactly what needed to be done to it, but I did recognize that it wasn't quite the finished article. It was certainly too long, and it also had some elements that were in their minds but hadn't translated so well to the page. For example, in the original script it wasn't clear to whom the dog Cofi belonged.

I had to also work out the dynamics of the relationship between Alejandro and Guillermo, because I hadn't seen a writer–director association like it before. They were very close and yet polar opposites. Because of this I was aware that there would be no room for a threesome, and that if I was going to work with them I would have to accept that I would be slightly on the outside. I can only describe the experience as being a little like working with two directors.

Francisco was initially a little apprehensive about my passion for the project, because he's much more practical than I am, and carried a huge responsibility at AltaVista in terms of the finances of the company. Both Francisco and I were quite young in relation to the amount of responsibility we had to assume on *Amores Perros* and I think Alejandro and Guillermo recognized this and were tolerant of it. Equally, Francisco and I were very tolerant of Alejandro and Guillermo through the creative process.

Alejandro Soberón read Guillermo's script and, despite being blown away by it, was also concerned that it was too long. At the very beginning we decided that we were going to have to cut it and also made it clear that we were not going to start shooting until we were sure that we were not going to be shooting copious amounts of material that would be surplus to the finished picture. We couldn't take this risk.

FRANCISCO GONZÁLEZ COMPEÁN: The first draft of Guillermo Arriaga's script was 148 or so pages long. We read the script and we loved it and so we started to work on it with Guillermo and Alejandro González Iñárritu and this was quite a long process. We were very respectful of the talent and this was essential to us because one of our company mission statements was to work with only the best talent possible.

Alejandro Soberón was a little bit doubtful, but we had sold Alejandro to our money people on the strength of his background as a DJ and commercials director, convincing them of his huge ability to connect with people. We were convinced that we should do this film but it was a risk because it was an expensive film; the initial budget started at $1.4 million and it escalated from there. Anyway, I gave Alejandro Soberón a copy of the script to read one night and the next morning he told me that he had gone to sleep at 4 a.m. because he had not been able to stop reading it. He loved it and was adamant that we make it. In this, Alejandro González Iñárritu was quite lucky.

I would be dishonest if I said that the financial department was not worried all the way through the project but they were very supportive of the story and of Alejandro.

MARTHA SOSA: The structure was the one of the things that was really thrilling for us at AltaVista. I got it and I love William Faulkner, one of Arriaga's primary influences.

The main thing, however, at least for me, were the characters – and this came from listening to how Alejandro spoke so passionately about each one. Alejandro really wears his heart on his sleeve and so listening to him describe the characters was a beautiful experience. It was also important that Alejandro was a DJ and so used to speaking to people and making his thoughts and passions very clear. He is very convincing.

Of course. Alejandro's ambition was to establish himself as a director. Francisco's and my main responsibility was to the budget because we knew that Alejandro was difficult to handle in this regard and we didn't want to have any problems with him or with the investors. The investors had made it very clear that we could not go a single peso over $2 million. For a Mexican film this was a lot of money. Prior to *Amores Perros* the traditional budget of a Mexican film was between $1.2 and $1.5 million so this was quite a leap and a gigantic risk for AltaVista. Remember, after *Todo el poder* this was only the second film AltaVista had produced and *Todo el poder* was a very different film to *Amores Perros*. As a company AltaVista was also still very much an un-established outsider. Everybody was like: 'So they're going to start making films without knowing a thing about it?'

Francisco and I made it very clear to Alejandro and Guillermo that we felt that we could learn from them and slowly gained their confidence. It was not easy and initially they did give us quite a hard time. Remember, for the project of their lives, Alejandro and Guillermo were also taking a risk and expressing a mutual trust in believing in producers who were not as experienced as some in Mexico.

FRANCISCO GONZÁLEZ COMPEÁN: Alejandro was an outsider who came from commercials and AltaVista were also outsiders and this appalled some people. When we started doing films there was a lot of jealousy because one of our financial partners previously funded other films and other production companies, and so we were seen as cutting off a potential financial source.

ALEJANDRO GONZÁLEZ IÑÁRRITU: There was some resentment, yes, and I think that sadly this a basic emotion of human nature. It is a very destructive and terrible feeling. However, I think that there was more of a feeling of surprise because, as well as coming from the wrong side of the tracks, I also lacked academic credentials. People thought, 'Who does this guy think he is? He comes from the world of commercials? Oh my god! Let's put a cross on him!' I was breaking the rules and *Amores Perros* raised a lot of questions about the system. But a lot of institutions and ways of thinking were shaken, and that was a very positive after-effect of the film.

* * *

FRANCISCO GONZÁLEZ COMPEÁN: Alejandro always wanted to cast Gael García Bernal as Octavio. I had seen him in Antonio Urrutia's Academy Award-nominated short film *De tripas, corazón*, and I knew that this guy glowed like a star and should be in movies.

ALEJANDRO GONZÁLEZ IÑÁRRITU: I knew that he was the one for the part. I had worked with Gael a couple of years ago on a commercial and I have nothing but praise for him. So one of the first and most crucial decisions that a director makes in a film was to my advantage because of that. Gael didn't have any feature-film experience, but he was studying theatre in London and had acted in some TV soap operas when he was a child, because he's the son of two talented actors.[1]

GAEL GARCÍA BERNAL: Acting was the obvious pathway for me. When I was very little I used to think that I was meant to be an actor, so my parents must be actors. Of course, it's the other way around . . . But it does feel as if I was born into this, in a way. I started acting in plays when I was ten or eleven, with the knowledge that it was what I wanted to do. And I acted in plays and plays and plays . . . But films seemed a very faraway destination, just because of the lack of films being made in Mexico. Also, film-making is a very special club, in Mexico and in any country, and a very difficult club to gain entry to. As theatre actors, my parents weren't members of that club.

Then I did *El Abuelo y yo* (1992), my first – and last – soap opera. But it was great fun and a good way to start: I made lots of friends, some very good actors that I still work with. It was after seeing this that Antonio Urrutia called me up to work in *De tripas, corazón* in Guadalajara – where he and I are both from, and it was a film about a town near Guadalajara, so we knew exactly what we were talking about. It was incredible to be able to work in film, and from that moment on I knew it was what I wanted to do. But there

Amores Perros: Gael García Bernal as Octavio

[1] Patricia Bernal and José Ángel García.

still wasn't any real film industry to speak of, so I still thought that I would work in theatre and that would be it. It wasn't until *Amores Perros* came along that I started to see that there were some great opportunities.

When I first got the script I read it so quickly. The intensity that you see in the film right from the very beginning was also there in the writing. I was totally mesmerized by it and shocked by the pace of it. And it was well written and extremely moving and I just savoured each page. At that point I'd read maybe four film scripts – now I receive about a hundred a day; most of which are terrible. But *Amores Perros* had a magic that I can only compare to when you are a little kid and you go to watch a movie in a cinema and it feels like a really big deal. And I knew I wanted to be involved.

Alejandro has a talent for telling stories and when he tells something he really seduces you into it. You trust him instantly and there is no question of whether or not he will be able to pull it off. I cannot really nail it in words – but there is something about him that inspires confidence.

I loved the fact that there were so many ambiguities to Octavio, but this was also one of the scariest aspects, the fact that there was so much complexity. I remember initially feeling overwhelmed with all the possibilities of the character and feared that I would not be able to capture the different tones. I arrived just two weeks before shooting and so came into the production very cold and on the outside. Vanessa Bauche [Susana] and Marco Pérez [Ramiro] had already been rehearsing together for months. Vanessa, Marco and indeed Alejandro were incredibly supportive of me. It was this support and understanding that helped me understand the complexities.

ALEJANDRO GONZÁLEZ IÑÁRRITU: I was initially worried, because when we first started rehearsing Gael didn't seem to have much idea about who his character was. I remember that when he arrived on location he asked me if I thought that his character would play tennis in the afternoons and I remember saying, 'What are you thinking? This guy is from the lower class!'

Gael was a little lost because we had been communicating mainly by telephone and because of school commitments he arrived on location later than many of the other actors. I was worried. But then, he went out for one or two nights with a few guys and then he got it just like that. He began to talk with the right kind of slightly vulgar accent and underwent something of a surprise and almost instant metamorphosis. He was and is a natural and I was fascinated since the first day by the supernatural relation between him and the camera.

GAEL GARCÍA BERNAL: I went to those places and did a lot of fieldwork. But what was pivotal and cathartic in terms of my grasping the character was working with dogs. I trained with guard dogs and also with ex-fighting dogs and, man, at times I was shitting myself. What you see in the film is us grabbing the dogs by the cheeks to stop them fighting with the other dogs and this really was all we had as a means of controlling them. In some scenes they were muzzled, but not all and I can tell you that the dogs would go absolutely mad. It was shooting these scenes that I gained an understanding as to why such contests as dog-fighting and even bull-fighting exist. This is not to say that I agree or disagree with them, but these experiences taught me that these situations are not human control against beast, it is beast against beast and the power of instinct. You lose it in there for a nanosecond and you are gone. This served as a really strong metaphor for me to do the film and to get the character. It had to be instinctive otherwise it would explode and become a horrendous melodrama. It was pivotal to get this edge, to capture the essence of the fact that the choices this character makes may decide whether or not he lives.

* * *

ALEJANDRO GONZÁLEZ IÑÁRRITU: With regards to the visual style of *Amores Perros*, it was something that I was experimenting with long before the movie through some exercises that I did in my commercials. Rodrigo Prieto, Brigitte Broch and Martín Hernández have been working with me as a team and developing different explorations together for several years, so we understand each other almost telepathically. They know exactly what I like or don't like and what I'm interested in.

RODRIGO PRIETO *cinematographer:* I first met Alejandro when he was directing commercials. I got a call to go into his office to show him my demo reel. He liked it and we began to work together on television commercials. We developed a very good working relationship and also a very good friendship. I loved his way of working, his intensity and really thought that his visual sense was just incredible. I remember one day telling him that I wanted to be considered when he made his first feature film.

While he was finishing working on the script for *Amores Perros* he sent me a copy and I was completely shocked. After all the stylish commercials we had shot, I wasn't expecting a script that was so hard and dramatic. My first reaction was: 'Man, are people going to like this?' But Alejandro is known for that. He always takes these huge risks, which I guess is the secret of his success. To be honest, whatever the script had been, with Alejandro directing I would have done it. Again, Alejandro had his own preconception about me. He thought that I was only into beautiful images and that I wouldn't want to do something as gritty as *Amores Perros*. In fact, I was precisely ready for it; it was *exactly* what I wanted to do.

MARTHA SOSA: Alejandro and Rodrigo Prieto can read each other's minds and trust each other completely. Alejandro is a great talker whereas Rodrigo is much quieter because he always knows exactly what Alejandro is thinking. Anyway, the first day Rodrigo met with Alejandro after having read the script and before they had even begun to discuss their ideas of what the film should look like, they both appeared at the meeting with a Nan Goldin book. Without knowing it, they both were thinking along exactly the same lines. In fact Brigitte Broch, the production designer, made up a book with photographs by Nan Goldin plus some photographs taken during the location scouting by her and Alejandro.

BRIGITTE BROCH *production designer*: I had worked with Alejandro for years off and on doing commercials, so we knew each other quite well. However, doing the movie with him and Rodrigo Prieto opened up a world for me that I did not know: the way a team can work, the way three passions can converge and create together with each of us putting a new idea into the cooking pot that eventually stewed up the raw look of the film.

Nan Goldin's photography was a suggestion from Alejandro and Rodrigo and I totally fell for her work. In addition I used photo references from Mexican photographers, including Pablo Ortiz Monasterio who had edited *La ultima ciudad*. There was a lot of field research, where Alejandro personally participated. In front of Chivo's location we found a makeshift hut of an old man who went out with his cart to collect trash. We ended up using his backyard for the burning of the dogs. That is how close we were to our characters' realities. None of us was afraid of getting too close to these worlds that seem so shocking, even though once we were assaulted by a gang of kids with real pistols sticking in our faces. We just lived in the movie. I must say, it is a rewarding feeling to be able to share passion on a project – it is a bonding for life.

Mexico City is a melting pot and all extremes inhabit it. We just presented what we personally lived and researched. I am sure that being a foreigner, even after thirty-five years of living in this country, helps me to always have a fresh and astounding view on situations, people, details, colours and smells And yes, I exploit this.

RODRIGO PRIETO: We used other movies in terms of the visual look that we wanted, I remember that we were particularly blown away by Wong Kar-Wai's *Happy Together*.

ALEJANDRO GONZÁLEZ IÑÁRRITU: Rodrigo and I made a commercial together for a bank in which we really explored the potentials of the handheld camera and the bleach-bypass process. We love this commercial. The bleach-bypass really captured the light of Mexico City, especially given that we shot the commercial on a very grey and overcast day. Commercials for me were always exercises, a way of exploring methods and approaches that I could use in a feature film later.

The bleach-bypass process I find has a spiritual quality that I relate to and really love.

RODRIGO PRIETO: I was looking to have a different texture to each one of the stories, so when we were doing our testing I played around with every procedure you can imagine – bleach-bypass, cross-process, dirty-dupe printing. In the end we decided not to be so obvious in the difference. I particularly wanted to do El Chivo's story in cross-process and maybe do Valeria's story in a more normal style and use bleach-bypass for Octavio. Alejandro felt that it would look like three different movies and I think that he was right. We decided to go for the whole movie with the bleach-bypass, as we liked the way that the intense colours reproduced a little bit less intense but still kept their basic intensity. We also liked the contrasts and the way that the skin tones became a little bit more bleached. We also liked the way that the grain was enhanced. So, we decided to separate the stories in more subtle ways, with lens choice, camera movement and style. I think that the way we shot each story in terms of the choice of lenses represented the greatest difference.

What happens in bleach-bypass is that when the negative is developed, one of the last steps that it goes through is bleaching to clean the excess silver off the film. Then you fix it and you have your negative. In this case we skipped that bleaching process so that the negative retains the excess silver. This is what creates the contrast and grain enhancement. The silver highlight element is retained. It is not that you are ruining the negative itself, though I do remember that this was a major concern of the studio behind *Amores Perros*. They were very concerned because at that time the process was relatively experimental and Kodak wouldn't guarantee that the negative would sustain the process. When we were preparing to do it I had to call all sorts of people who were doing it at the time to make sure that we weren't going to ruin the negative. I think David O. Russell's *Three Kings* was one such production. Alejandro, again being a risk-taker, always thought that we should go for it and that the risk element would be worth it.

* * *

ALEJANDRO GONZÁLEZ IÑÁRRITU: The second segment was difficult to shoot, mainly because it took us into other genres apart from drama. I mean, it has moments of comedy and also of surreal farce. The whole thing seems absurd, even when it was a real story that happened to a friend of mine when we were eleven years old. In the real story, things were worse, because the apartment began to smell terrible and the puppy was dead. To tell you the truth, this segment was in its entirety one hour and fifty-eight minutes, and as a stand-alone piece worked perfectly. However, as part of the whole it jarred.

RODRIGO PRIETO: Logistically the shoot was often a nightmare. For example, for the car-crash scene we had to close off a street for three consecutive Sundays. It was also very tricky because we didn't have the budget to do the accident twice; we just had one take with nine cameras. On the day that we were preparing for it, it started to rain and the road became very slippery. During one of the rehearsals the car actually struck another car when we weren't shooting. We had to repair the car, all the while very aware that the light was fading. We also had a man who refused to move his taxi out of the street and just left it there. Of course, when the crash happened, one of the cars just went straight into the taxi.

ALEJANDRO GONZÁLEZ IÑÁRRITU: It was very hard. I had to shoot the car chase in just one day, and the car crash in half of a day. We were pulling the car using electric power and the people were furious in the streets. The police were there to help, but were not really helping us. The day we shot the crash we had nine cameras and the sun was beginning to go down and the whole situation was becoming very dangerous. The video assist projecting the nine cameras was off because of a technical problem. Rodrigo Prieto and I were running from one angle to another like crazy. That same day in the morning we shot the scene of the bank robbery and we were exhausted. The car that was hit travelled a hundred metres without control and people were desperate to see what was happening despite our pleas for them to stay clear and keep out of the way. The car was travelling at a hundred kilometres per hour and ended up accidentally hitting a taxi that was parked near by and nearly killing a hundred people that were two metres from that taxi without security. It was insane. I will never forget the sound of that crash and the braveness of Emilio Echevarría ('the goat') who knew the danger he was running being in front of that car where nobody knew exactly what would happen after the other car hit it at forty miles per hour. You would never see this kind of car crash on film in the United States. The shot and the whole set-up were very risky which also makes it feel so real.

RODRIGO PRIETO: The sequence where Octavio has Cofi bleeding on his back seat was very uncomfortable, particularly as I was crouched right next to a dog that was asleep and covered in blood. It was very sticky and extremely hot. It may not look like it but I had a lot of lighting in there to bring the levels up and to ensure that we could still see outside of the car and still see the other car following. Also, to be able to see the black dog with the bleach-bypass process I had to really pump a lot of light into the car. I was there sweating with a camera covered in blood and myself getting very smelly.

ALEJANDRO GONZÁLEZ IÑÁRRITU: People say that *Amores Perros* is very stylish but I do not think that this is true. You and I and every human being see the world in hand-held. In other words, we look and move our heads. My head and eyes have never been mounted on a crane, a dolly or a tripod. Those things are stylish and unnatural to our relationship with the world. The approach is both more intimate and more real.

RODRIGO PRIETO: Absolutely all of the film is shot hand-held. Even when El Chivo calls his daughter and leaves a message on her answerphone. I was inside a closet with the camera on my knee and I was looking through the finder. It was very difficult to operate. The camera is static, but it breathes. This was our philosophy behind a lot of the movie because there are other static shots where the camera is either on my shoulder or on my knee. There are certain shots where we placed the camera on a sandbag but we always wanted it to be slightly moving, as if it were breathing. We wanted to give a sense of witnessing things.

That particular scene with El Chivo I couldn't stop crying myself because I have two daughters and it was very emotional. He was talking about leaving his daughter and with my line of work I am often away from home for long periods and feel so much guilt for being away and seemingly abandoning my family. At this moment it really got to me and I was even starting to fog up the viewfinder. I could hardly keep myself from sobbing.

The same thing happened to me on *21 Grams* – twice in fact. Alejandro has this capacity and really does go straight to the heart.

There are several moments that stay in mind as very characteristic of *Amores Perros*. One is the scene where Octavio and Susana are talking and she confesses that she is pregnant again, and Octavio offers to run away with her. There is a close up of Gael that when we were filming Gael went way past the mark where he was expected to go and came so close to the camera that it went out of focus. As he passed the camera I panned to follow him. Technically the scene is wrong – in the movie you can actually see a stand from some equipment – but emotionally it is so charged. I love this shot and never for one moment did I dare say, 'We have to do this again.' The fact that it went out of focus because he went out of focus and caught us off guard gives it more power. It is exciting for me to see things happen that I didn't expect and then just let them be.

I try more and more to allow the actors to do their thing. I try not to put very specific marks on the floor and give them exact directions. I prefer it when a movie has more emotional impact; the photography is often better as well, even if sometimes it may have technical defects. I have obviously worked on movies where everything is compositionally exact and I hate it when people say to me, 'You know, the movie wasn't very good but the photography is great.' My reaction is that if that's the case then it wasn't worth it. I don't care to do beautiful photography on bad movies.

It was very scary being in a little arena amongst these dogs operating a hand-held camera. There were trainers, who were out of shot of course, and apart from the Rottweilers the other dogs, I was told, would attack only other dogs and not a human. However, I still decided to wear a security blanket. It was frightening but I think that the danger in the finished film comes across as a result of the sound and the editing. The dogs were muzzled so that they could not open their mouths when they were actually fighting but of course in the film there are all these shots of the dogs barking and baring their teeth. There is a kind of montage mêlée of this barking that goes on for something like fifteen frames that is very disquieting. We did go to actual dogfights on scouting missions to get a sense of the atmosphere and the ambience and I can tell you that it was upsetting and really horrible. The fights are slow and take a long time but the dogs are not allowed to kill each other. The fight ends when one dog gives up.

* * *

ALEJANDRO GONZÁLEZ IÑÁRRITU: The film changed a lot in post-production because it had to. It was always changing. I believe that film is very much a living thing and should always be susceptible to even the subtlest of changes. If water doesn't run, it smells bad . . .

MARTHA SOSA: You are probably going to hear several versions about this because nobody can agree . . .

First of all, Francisco and myself were inexperienced producers, scared to death because we had gone over budget. Our investors had made a number of key stipulations, including that Alejandro stick to the script, that the film have a strong contemporary soundtrack – and that Alejandro remain on budget. Should he go over budget, the investors made it a point of contract that he would have to pay for it personally. They also insisted on retaining final cut, so, despite what you may hear to the contrary, Alejandro did not have final cut on *Amores Perros*. We happened to agree with almost all of the creative decisions that Alejandro and Guillermo made. It was after we went over budget that things started to get a little complicated, and I think that Alejandro felt that our belief in him was starting to waver. I couldn't make the investors change their mind, though I tried very hard, so as not to make Alejandro pay for the over-budget. It was too painful. It was like having my heart broken, because on the one hand I could see something really magical happening with the film he was making, but on the other hand I realized that when he was on Take 20 of a scene this could seriously affect the whole production and was outside of our agreement. I can't tell you how hard it was. I wanted to see what he was looking for, and often Take 20 was the best one. The thing about working with a genius is that there is a high price to pay, but it's also so unbelievable what he can achieve.

I think the film, perhaps out of a sense of growing insecurity, was then screened to too many people to get advice. Some of those willing to offer advice really cared for Alejandro and for his film, while others were simply envious and so apt to offer counsel that was destructive. It was at this time that Alejandro asked if he could edit the film in his home, because he hadn't seen his children for so long. I was so touched by this request, despite the fact that others saw it as his means of effectively kidnapping the film.

Guillermo del Toro then offered his assistance and expertise.

GUILLERMO DEL TORO *director*: I didn't know Alejandro back then but Alfonso Cuarón had told me that I should see *Amores Perros*. I saw it and called Alejandro to tell him that he had made a masterpiece but that it was twenty minutes too long . . .

ALEJANDRO GONZÁLEZ IÑÁRRITU: We began a series of intense telephone conversations, with him calling me every day at 7 a.m. He had a lot of very radical ideas, including taking out the majority of the second story, to which I replied, 'Fuck you, who do you think you are?' At this time del Toro was in Spain during the production of *The Devil's Backbone*. He flew to Mexico and knocked on my door. I opened it and he said, 'Hi, I'm Guillermo del Toro', and then he spent three days with me working on the film and sleeping on my floor. He also ate everything that he found in my house.

By that time, I had already spent seven months editing the film alone in my house and even when I was really happy and very, very close, I knew that I should cut it a little bit more but didn't know how. During this time we had a lot of discussions as, at the time, the film was almost two hours and forty minutes long. Guillermo really helped me to pare it down another seven minutes, and encouraged me and told me not to be afraid. I really appreciated this, as there are times when as the director you can begin to lose your perspective. Guillermo has the mind of a producer too, and I really believe in him. I don't always believe producers and always tend to produce my own things, but the fact that he is also a director meant that I was able to trust him. He and Carlos Bolado helped me at the end to reduce the fat that is so often simply left in films.

FRANCISCO GONZÁLEZ COMPEÁN: I remember thinking that the film needed cutting but Alejandro felt that he had reached a dead end with it so we did a test screening – something which was at the time rarely done in Mexico – and after seeing it with an audience Alejandro and Guillermo Arriaga emerged and admitted that it still needed cutting just a little more. When you are sitting with a hundred strangers watching your film you immediately know if it is too long. And Alejandro saw how the film played and naturally came to the conclusion that he needed to trim it a little more.

MARTHA SOSA: The most important thing to me was not the running time; it was the ending. In the script and in Alejandro's original ending, the film concludes on two gunshots heard outside El Chivo's house. I felt that this ending was very unfair and quite false, as it didn't reflect any possibility of hope. Also, the two corrupt brothers, the Cain and Abel of the story, are not main characters and, in their selfishness and willingness to kill each other, very difficult to care about. I felt that it was very important to finish on two of the main characters of the film, El Chivo and Cofi, the dog that had so dramatically changed the course of his life. I wasn't the one who was able to convince Alejandro to make the change, but I was one of those obsessed with the ending. Actually, I think that we have to thank Alejandro's wife Maria Eladia for the concluding glimpse of salvation, because she had a similar response to Alejandro's original conclusion and quietly suggested to Alejandro that perhaps he ought to at least contemplate other possibilities.

ALEJANDRO GONZÁLEZ IÑÁRRITU: Guillermo visited me during the shoot with his family for a week or so. Then he saw the final cut. Fortunately, even with some of the changes and scenes that I had to take out or move around, he froze for a couple of hours, but then he seemed to like it.

MARTHA SOSA: Cannes was very important because it gave us the opportunity to launch the film very successfully in Mexico. This may seem something of a paradox, but a very tough, two-and-a-half-hour film had to be

© Altavista Films

Amores Perros: Emilio Echevarría as political assassin El chivo

accompanied by something extraordinary, especially as we weren't in the Official Selection but the Critics' Week. So we created something extraordinary, spinning an aura around the film and its Cannes experience, to make it seem much bigger than it actually was. From a Mexican perspective we made it look as if we'd won the World Cup. You have to remember that at this time we were trying to grab new audiences and were asking people to give us the opportunity to show them that we could make good films that they could identify with and be proud of. We needed to create a lot of noise and you cannot do that with advertising alone.

We also had very good reflexes. Alejandro Soberón and Federico may not have had a long track record in terms of producing an international film such as *Amores Perros* but they knew that they had to profit from the moment. NuVisión, the Mexican distributor of the film and so the company responsible for deciding how much would be put into the film's prints and advertising campaign, just really didn't get it. On seeing *Amores Perros* before it screened in Cannes, NuVisión said that they felt that the film was well made but needed more cutting, especially the middle story. They also outlined their plans to release the film in Mexico on forty prints. As soon as I heard these comments I knew that we were going to have a very big fight. Fortunately, Alejandro Soberón and Federico knew that the distributor was wrong, and after winning the Critics' Week Grand Prize in Cannes were able to successfully argue against releasing the film in August, NuVisión's original plan, and insisted on it being released in June, as a big summer picture. Post Cannes, *Amores Perros* was released on over two hundred prints.[2] So, in terms of luck, strategy and prestige, Cannes was a very good moment.

I believe that the audiences, and especially the younger ones, were eager to see something different. I also believe that Alejandro has the ability to turn everything he touches into gold. I also consider him one of the best salesmen you will ever meet and the work that he did to publicize the film in terms of giving interviews and doing Q&As was phenomenal; even the media were seduced by this.

You have to remember that when Alejandro made the film he was already very successful. If you are a successful person in Mexico and you offer a portrayal of poor people and the way they live their life there will be a certain amount of resentment. What Alejandro did very intelligently point out was that he was not born rich; that his father worked hard for a living and that he grew up in a so-so neighbourhood. Alejandro has made no secret of the fact that he has climbed the social ladder but he did not begin at the top of it. Arriaga is the same. They were both forced to justify their right to offer these representations and talk about the poor and to their credit they did it.

What is important is that the film appeared in a very specific moment and we were lucky. We are good at marketing . . . but not geniuses. At the moment the film appeared, every single young person in Mexico was thinking about the kind of changes they wanted to see in Mexico and the ways in which they could make a difference. Once *Amores Perros* was launched you could see two things very clearly throughout the city: the *Amores Perros* marketing campaign and Vicente Fox's political campaign.

FRANCISCO GONZÁLEZ COMPEÁN: Remember that Alejandro is a partner in a very important advertising agency, and so put his entire advertising infrastructure together with ours. We had a great team including Richard Ham

[2] Released on 215 prints on 16 August 2000 by NuVisión, a sister company of AltaVista, *Amores Perros* grossed approximately $8.8 million at the Mexican box office. This currently makes it the fourth-highest-grossing Mexican film in Mexico of all time.

who was the head of marketing for Fox Latin America and really put his all into *Amores Perros*. Alejandro was personally involved in making the trailers, which often led to very lively discussions but with teamwork we got there in the end.

It's important to note that the typical publicity and advertising budget for a film in Mexico was $50–$70,000 at most. With *Amores Perros* we spent $1.1 million. It's all about competing and getting the film out there and making sure that everybody knows about it. This is the aspect that I am very closely involved with.

MARTHA SOSA: I think that *Amores Perros* has become a very focal point of reference. I mean this in many ways, mainly in the quality of the film. It has also undeniably become a point of reference in the whole question of how a film is manufactured, marketed and then launched.

FRANCISCO GONZÁLEZ COMPEÁN: A lot of the research and thinking we conducted did address the question of how we could make our films fly outside of Mexico. There are two ways to do this. One is to give a false impression, as in *Como agua para chocolate* (1991). People saw that film and thought of Mexico as so romantic and so passionate and full of magical food and love. The other way to do it is to shock them, be different, play with the structure and be formally audacious. *Amores Perros* is completely daring, fresh and different and when people saw it they went, 'Wow!'

ALEJANDRO GONZÁLEZ IÑÁRRITU: I was completely surprised. That said, when I was editing the film during seven months in my house I knew I had something that had the capacity to touch the hearts of people and I knew that it captured life. But, I never imagined how people would react to it. I also was surprised by the reaction to the film outside of Mexico because at this time I had no idea of the bigger picture of cinema. I hadn't been to festivals and wasn't a cineaste; I was just a guy who happened to like films. I had no perception of the film within the world so it was overwhelming for me when *Amores Perros* took the place that it did within the cinema world.

MARTHA SOSA: One of the things I adore about living in Mexico City is the huge contrast. But it's hard and painful. *Amores Perros* certainly captures Mexico City as a place of contrast in a time of change but perhaps reflects only a belief as to what Mexico is like as opposed to depicting the reality of what it is like.

ALEJANDRO GONZÁLEZ IÑÁRRITU: It is a very Mexican film. I avoid showing the city and show very few landmarks. There is nothing that you can recognize from Mexico City and yet it captures the smell and essence of the city. Without pointing a political finger, the film is also through its characters and their situations a very political film and is inherently Mexican. I feel very proud of that. I travel everywhere and when people ask me where I am from and I say Mexico, without knowing that I am the director they say that they have seen *Amores Perros*, a film that for them crystallizes Mexico and three or four years after lives in their minds. It has become synonymous with Mexico. To me this is fucking unbelievable. I wanted to portray a fascinating and complex place without wishing to patronize, diminish or insult it. Unfortunately, there were some Mexican cultural ambassadors who felt that *Amores Perros* degraded Mexico throughout the world. This was the case with the Mexican cultural attaché in Japan who refused to screen my film even after I won Best Director and Best Film for the first time in the history of the Tokyo Film Festival. That's the classical Mexican political stupidity.

ÁNGELES CASTRO *Director,* CCC: I believe that maybe because of the overwhelming influence of American cinema, and because of the influence of the 'Golden Age' of Mexican cinema, it has become very difficult to look at ourselves now. It seems that if the films were not filled with Mexican cowboys or singers, then from the 1960s there were only isolated examples of films that seemed to work in terms of offering an authentic representation. *Amores Perros* reveals a reality, but it reveals only an urban reality. This reality is of course not the same across the whole country. The fact that *Amores Perros* was set in a city was, I believe, integral to its international success. Cities can be treated in a very universal way and urban themes and concerns can be very easily transmitted to other cultures.

GAEL GARCÍA BERNAL: I think Mexico City has never before been so alive on film before and that even just a single frame of that film says so much about society and social status and also about lives and loves and passions. It makes you embark on a journey. I am also moved by the energy and blunt uncompromising nature of the film. It speaks volumes about a film-maker doing what he wants and is also a very abrupt example of the value of teamwork in the film-making process.

I suppose that people react in a positive way to something that is good, especially when it is something from their own country and so a source from which they can take pride. What you must also consider besides the obvious quality of the film was that it was so refreshing to have a Mexican film that did not treat the Mexican audience like idiots. In Mexico we love to watch films and I personally really love to watch films but I don't need marketing gimmicks to tell me what is good and what is valuable. I myself and people in general in Mexico forged a real connection with this film. They became a part of it and came to feel almost as if they owned their own small piece of it.

Outside Mexico it is perhaps a little easier to explain. The success of the film at festivals was very important, as was the fact that it more or less came from nowhere, or rather from a place that for the previous few years had not had any kind of cinematic spark. It was highly recommended at festivals, Cannes especially, and I think that when people did see it after numerous recommendations they were pleasantly surprised.

I remember arriving in Cannes for the film. I hadn't at that point seen it and like many of us from the film who had made the trip, I didn't even have a hotel room. It was also for many of us our first film experience. The whole trip was crazy, going to parties and meeting people, but from the moment that the film won,[3] our lives changed. I mean of course the lives of those involved in the film but I also refer to those involved in the Mexican film industry.

GUILLERMO ARRIAGA: When they released *Amores Perros* in Mexico, Alejandro and I would often turn up unannounced at the theatres and ask the managers if we could go up and talk to the audiences afterwards. We would listen to the opinions of the audiences and they would all thank us for the film because they were sick of being fed stupid urban comedies. They appreciated the fact that they were able to see themselves on screen.

I think that *Amores Perros* taught film-makers and producers to take bigger risks and to show more respect for the audiences. I think that film-makers are no longer scared of touching on these more realistic themes. It is also a film that played well to audiences of all ages and classes. Despite the prohibitive cost of going to the cinema in Mexico, almost everyone went to see it. People had a reconciliation with Mexican cinema. It is also a very contradictory film, it shows Mexico and Mexicans as ugly but sometimes we are and we are also tired of trying to live up to the fantasy of a soap-opera world.

BERTHA NAVARRO: González Iñárritu brought to the project a vast knowledge of film-making. It certainly doesn't look like a first film.

CARLOS CUARÓN *screenwriter/director*: The first time I saw *Amores Perros* I had to bow to Alejandro. I saw it in the editing stage and I thought, 'Wow, this is new!'

[3] At the 2000 Cannes Film Festival *Amores Perros* won the Critics' Week Grand Prize and was awarded the Young Critics' Award for Best Feature.

LEONARDO GARCÍA TSAO *critic/academic*: I think that what was perhaps most interesting about *Amores Perros* was that it was privately funded. Stylistically, yes, it took some risks but not too many. The Jorge Fons film *Midaq Alley* (1994) had a very similar structure. It starts with one action, the playing of dominoes, and then moves on to encounter different characters and narratives in that way. *Amores Perros* is certainly more indebted to this film than to *Pulp Fiction*, which everybody was so quick to compare it to. Arriaga, I think, really used *Midaq Alley* as a model in terms of structure.

Don't get me wrong, *Amores Perros* is extremely well done, and it is amazing that a first film can have such energy and drive. It creates a potent sense of atmosphere and is a really important film for capturing the characteristics of Mexico City at the turn of the century. It avoids stereotypes, and moves through many social classes, never marginalizing either the working or middle classes. I thought that it was also important to show the former guerrilla fighter who is now completely on the margins of society but, because of his daughter, is torn by the notion of trying to find his way back. That was very telling of the moment.

I think its success was a combination of the film appealing to a younger demographic; its visual panache and its ability to capture the Zeitgeist in terms of a general dissatisfaction with the social and political situation in Mexico. It certainly came out at the right moment and it had an unprecedented advertising campaign. I can think of few films before this that had such a huge advertising campaign. It was on every billboard and on the side of every bus. There was also heavy support from the media in general, specifically television and radio. It was impossible to miss it. Audiences in Mexico are very fickle and unpredictable. But it was a film that built huge expectations and somehow managed to fulfil them.

At the same time I know that, although it broke even, *Amores Perros* didn't turn a profit. They had spent so much that the box-office earnings barely covered it. It's a very high-risk game and the stakes are getting so high that it is becoming ridiculous.

Amores Perros *is the winner of over thirty international awards and is among the most decorated films in the history of Mexican cinema. Nominated in the best Foreign Film category at both the Golden Globes and the Academy Awards, the film won the Cannes Critics' Week prize; a* BAFTA *for Best Film not in the English Language and a New Directors Award at the Edinburgh International Film Festival. At the Ariels (the prestigious Mexican equivalent of the Academy Awards), the film triumphed in a brace of categories including Best Director, Best Actor (Gael García Bernal), Best Cinematography and Best Editing. The film was also presented with the Golden Ariel.*

GUILLERMO DEL TORO: I think that audiences are incredibly hungry to see themselves in movies that go beyond what they were previously used to, the dumb comedies, the soaps and the like. They want to see themselves in that car wreck in *Amores Perros*. For better or for worse there is a level of excitement that Alejandro gives to his images, and a level of excitement among audiences in saying, 'That's the street where I work!' or 'There's the street where I live!' And there's certainly a level of excitement in recognizing yourself in a genre situation. Beyond the social exploration of *Amores Perros*, the foremost characteristic of that movie is the sheer level of adrenalin. It's a non-stop ride in your hometown that gives such a high. Why do all the chases have to happen in Manhattan? Why do all the exciting things have to happen in America? Why can we not have exciting things happen here in Mexico?

ROSA BOSCH: There is a theory, and I'm not necessarily saying that I subscribe to it, that the popularity boom experienced in the last ten years or so of the soap opera or *telenovela* has rekindled in Mexico the appetite for local stories. I think there is a young generation who want to see local stuff.

ALFREDO JOSKOWICZ: In art, you have no moral conclusions. If it works, it gives you a strong emotion and that's it . . . It is very complicated; we are very proud of the new democracy we have, but we still do not have a clear national patriotic direction. Feelings are intricate, and the newer directors and producers are looking to feed into this and give a stronger emotion. There is also a new phenomenon in the arts generally, and especially I feel in cinema, in that the author or the director now feels that they can really say whatever it is that they want to say. They can do this even if they have received financial assistance or help from the state. There is a feeling of liberation.

ROSA BOSCH: I also think there's a certain element of backlash against Hollywood. Mexico now has its own stars, and I'm thinking specifically here of Gael and Diego. So why should Mexicans go and see only films with run-of-the-mill American stars? There is also a sense of a renewed pride in our national product. For many years, and this is also the case in Spain, local films were considered inferior, they were perhaps not well made, certainly cheaply made, and they didn't have any 'hip' factor. It certainly wasn't hip to take your girlfriend on a Friday night to see a Mexican film. Now, this is exactly what you would do.

FRANCISCO GONZÁLEZ COMPEÁN: There have been a lot of repercussions from *Amores Perros*. It showed Mexican film-makers and producers that you could make a very strong, daring film, and still be successful at the box office. Another major repercussion was that it showed our Mexican directors working in the US that they could come back to Mexico and still make a challenging and successful personal project. I am, of course, directly referring to Alfonso Cuarón and *Y tu mamá también*; and indirectly to Guillermo del Toro and *The Devil's Backbone*. I'm not saying that Alfonso decided to do *Y tu mamá también* only after seeing *Amores Perros*. But it must have helped . . .

5
Y tu mamá también and *The Devil's Backbone*

In 2000 the Mexican political landscape changed once more, with repercussions in due course for the national cinema. For seventy years Mexican politics had been dominated by the Institutional Revolutionary Party (PRI), but the 1997 parliamentary elections saw the combined opposition win more support, thus breaking what was in effect a one-party system with a democratic façade. The 2000 presidential elections confirmed the development, as Vicente Fox of the National Action Party (PAN) beat the PRI candidate by more than 6 per cent of the vote.

Sensing Fox's impending victory and a potential for change, democracy and reform, Mexicans had been swept along on a euphoric wave of optimism. Fox assumed the presidency in December, following a high-profile and extensive media campaign aimed at attracting younger voters. He promised sweeping reforms, including better distribution of income in Mexico and an overhaul of state institutions.

Alfredo Joskowicz was appointed Director of the Mexican Film Institute (IMCINE) in December 2000, and immediately had to get to grips with administering a budget that included much coveted production funds.

ALFREDO JOSKOWICZ *film-maker/Director,* IMCINE: I took up my position in January 2001. It's very hard work. I'm fighting. But I think my background has been very important, because I understand all the difficulties of the sector.

IMCINE has two substantial areas: the direction of support towards production, and the promotion of Mexican cinema both in Mexico and throughout the world. Promotion is the significant area, and annually we have a national contest for aspiring and developing writers. We invite projects and make a selection of those to which we can give financial assistance for development. We also have a national contest for short films, and we are able to place the winners on the front of commercial features, so that they can play in theatres. It also makes the films easier to position at international festivals and we receive a lot of recognition and prizes for our shorts. We don't receive any extra subsidies for this, but our aim is to put into position and nurture new actors, writers, directors etc. With regard to feature films, we have two government funds. The first, FIDECINE received $7 million in 2000, around 70 million pesos. This money was received at the end of 2000 so was used towards features being made in 2001. At the end of 2001 another $7 million was made available, this will go to features being produced in 2002. With these FIDECINE funds we supported sixteen films in two years.

We have another older fund that was created in 1998 because in this year local feature production was very low. In 1997 Mexico produced only nine feature films, the lowest number since 1932 so the government was compelled to help; FOPROCINE was created to assist quality films. In the last five years, we have used FOPROCINE funds to assist forty-seven films in the last five years. The government put $13.5 million into FOPROCINE, a fund that was responsible for *Sexo, pudor y lágrimas* (1999), a film that attracted an audience of 5.3 million people. *El crimen del padre Amaro* (2002), another FOPROCINE-assisted film also achieved over 5 million viewers in Mexico and has gone on to be the most successful Mexican film in our history. Unfortunately, even with these successes the fund is not enough and the $13.5 million has not been recouped. The FOPROCINE fund comes to an end in 2003 so from 2004 FIDECINE is the only fund that will exist.

To be relatively proportionate you cannot give all of the money to one or two films so the FIDECINE rules dictate that you can give only a maximum of $700,000 per film or 49 per cent of the total budget. Private producers therefore have to provide 51 per cent of the budget. If we consider the fact that the average cost of a film in Mexico is now $1.5 million, then even with FIDECINE funding of $700,000, the private producer still has to raise $800,000, which is very difficult. People say that this is market forces but this doesn't take into account the distribution of the peso at the Mexican box office. Fifteen cents is tax. Fifty-one cents is for the exhibitor. Thirty-four cents goes to the distributor. From this the distributor will recoup the cost of prints and advertising. After recouping these costs the distributor gives to the producer thirteen cents and retains twenty-nine cents. The producer, the one who raises the finance for the film and takes all the risks, is right at the very end of the chain. This is a major problem and not only in Mexico but throughout Latin American countries. What the governments in other Latin American territories have done is instigate tax incentives and channelled money from television and video distribution back into cinema production. Argentina, for example, raised $25 million dollars last year in this way and can now produce fifty to sixty films annually. We must remember that they are doing this despite a period of severe economic depression. In Mexico we do not have such taxes for cinema.

JOSÉ LUIS GARCÍA AGRAZ *director*: A producer can't receive money from both funds; it's either one or the other. In this second fund there are fewer dignitaries and the committee comprises representatives of sectors such as distribution, the cinema owners and the trade unions – this committee is supposed to have a more 'commercial' vision.

The truth of the matter is that it's not enough, and that you do have to look for co-producers among the 'Anglospoken' – the US, the UK, Australia, Canada – among whom the hardest to find are the Americans . . .

* * *

CARLOS CUARÓN *writer/director*: In 1997 I started directing short films I had written,[1] and in 2000 I was going to make my first feature but the production collapsed. In hindsight I'm grateful, because I wasn't ready to direct it – the script wasn't ready; the producers weren't ready. And because of that, I sat down with Alfonso and wrote *Y tu mamá también.*

ALFONSO CUARÓN *director*: My son was in New York and we'd go to movies together all the time; sometimes I would choose the movie, and other times he would. And basically I had to see a lot of crap, and a lot of teen comedies. The problem with the teen comedies is that there's something really interesting at their core: they're so moralistic and they have a phoney and overly respectful sense of character. You don't have to make fun of the characters or invent clever plots to humiliate one or the other, or have them sticking their dicks into a pie. I was lucky, because when my son was ten I made *A Little Princess*, which, in a way, was a film for me; and then I wanted to do a teen movie for him because of course he ended up being a teen. This movie was *Y tu mamá* and in many ways I used my son as an adviser. Ultimately my son is very Mexican – even living in New York he's very Mexican and he sees that the fundamentals and the emotions between teens – most of his friends are American – are basically the same. The politics may be different but the human experience is ultimately the same, they are all insecure, they all want to bed women and they are all in love with the girl who loves the other guy.

Carlos and I had talked about the ideas of *Y tu mamá* even before *Sólo con tu pareja*. We were looking for a low-budget film to do before my first film. Lubezki suggested a road trip to the beach, and Carlos loved the idea of two

[1] Perhaps the best known of these, *Me la debes* (*You Owe Me*), is included on the UK DVD of *Y tu mamá también.*

boys and one girl. For various reasons we moved on into *Sólo con tu pareja*. But, every couple of years, Carlos and I would return to it before putting it back in the drawer. It was in this way that it evolved.

Directors are really perhaps only as good as the projects they choose. And choices can be dangerous, because you can lose sight of what you really want to do. What happened to me was that I was choosing so many projects that I forgot that I could write. And that was part of the beauty of *Y tu mamá*.

EMMANUEL LUBEZKI *cinematographer*: I remember when Alfonso and I were working on *Great Expectations* and we were both so fed up and having trouble finding the energy and enthusiasm to like our work any more. We both felt that *Y tu mamá también* was a way of reinventing ourselves.

GUILLERMO DEL TORO *director*: I think that a career is a learning curve. Alfonso and I have discussed this many times. I remember Alfonso being revered as a visionary when *A Little Princess* came out and maligned as a

Y tu mamá también: Dirty Dancing – Diego Luna, Maribel Verdú, Gael García Bernal

hack when *Great Expectations* emerged. I went through similar stuff with *Cronos* and *Mimic*, and I said to Alfonso, 'People seem to think that you are making a definitive last statement with every movie. It's not the case; you are searching, in the way that a painter may experiment with a blue period or a green period.

ALFONSO CUARÓN: I didn't do *Y tu mamá* to go 'back home'; I did the film in Mexico because I always wanted to make it. I never really intended to go to Hollywood, and I don't regard it as the Mecca of cinema. For many directors, Mexican or otherwise, it's a goal; for some others it is just part of a journey. For me, personally, it's the latter. I want to do films elsewhere and everywhere.

Some film-makers don't need to touch Hollywood. Guillermo del Toro is clear: when he does his Hollywood movies, he isn't pretending to do his smaller movies, and vice versa; they are two different approaches and two different beasts.

When I did *Y tu mamá* I did feel that I had perhaps started to lose some of my identity and that I needed to reconnect with my roots – not bullshit nationalistic roots but creative roots. I wanted to make the film I was going to make before I went to film school, and that was always going to be a film in Spanish, and a road movie involving a journey to the beach. All the rest, Mexico versus the big Hollywood giants, is ideology. I have very eclectic tastes in terms of film, and I want to explore these.

Great Expectations, if it was successful or not is not for me to say, but it's obviously a completely different film to *Y tu mamá*; it has an entirely different point of view. The same with *A Little Princess* – I was following the point of view of the main character. Our approach, mine and Lubezki's, on these films was not to see the world the way it is, but the way it is perceived by the protagonists – to give a heightened reality, almost. On *Y tu mamá* we wanted to do the opposite: an objective approach to our reality, just to keep our distance and observe things happening.

Carlos and I didn't find a way into the film until around 2000, when we decided that the context was as important as character and that we wanted a very objective and in some ways *distant* approach to the story. We didn't want to take a nostalgic approach.

Abandoned by their girlfriends for the summer, the well-heeled Tenoch (Diego Luna) and barrio *boy Julio (Gael García Bernal) meet beautiful, thirtyish Luisa (Maribel Verdú) at a wedding. Luisa's marriage to Tenoch's cousin is in bad shape. The teenagers seek to impress her by boasting that they are about to embark on a road trip to an idyllic but barely known beach called Boca del Cielo ('Heaven's Mouth'). They are surprised when Luisa asks if she can accompany them, and soon the unlikely trio are headed out of Mexico City. The journey (widely seen as an allegory as well as a literal excursion) brings sexual gratification and rivalry for the boys and a lesson in Mexico's geography, as well as its socio-economic context, for the viewer.*

CARLOS CUARÓN: We were kind of blocked in the writing and got ourselves stuck with a narrator. He doesn't actually narrate that much; rather, he contextualizes. And we decided that context – in this case, Mexico, as a country – was character. When we discovered this early structuring, we decided that it was a parallel trip. The woman's journey is also important, because she too is finding her own identity, perhaps in a much more Spanish way. But, yeah, the two guys are searching for an identity. And I still feel that Mexico is still a teenage society. The difference, I believe, is that the society is much more mature than the government. We are sixteen, seventeen, and pimply and in the middle of the teenage years. And my feeling is that the government is about thirteen and just starting with the hormonal thing . . .

EMMANUEL LUBEZKI: It couldn't be just a coming-of-age story and nothing else. The context is so important, and it's actually a very complex movie told in quite a simple way – that's what really blew me away. A friend of us who lived with us in Mexico when we were growing up but then moved back to Uruguay wrote to me to say that the film really helped him understand who we were, and how sex was so important to us that, despite our leftist sympathies, it blinded us to the situations that were going on around us. Sadly, Mexico is now such a complex country that if you and a girl were to head to the interstate in a car the chances are that you would be robbed and raped.

ALFONSO CUARÓN: The story wasn't autobiographical, but there are elements from when Carlos and I were growing up. The nanny in the film is played by our nanny in real life, and one of the destinations the trio go through is her town in real life; Carlos and I went to a wedding in the same place where you see the wedding in the film, and the President of the time was present and everybody was more interested in the President than the newlyweds. We also had a car like the one in the film and there is a town the trio visit that is also the name of the street where we grew up. The character of Diego 'Saba' Madero, the friend of Julio and Tenoch, is a character that we know. Of course, we both also had trips to the beach and the incident with the pigs in the tent happened to my cinematographer, Emmanuel Lubezki. There's lots of incidental stuff like that. I think that both Carlos and I are in between

Julio and Tenoch – leaning more towards Julio, I guess, socially speaking. What we really wanted to do was convey a universe and an atmosphere that we really knew first hand.

CARLOS CUARÓN: It was mainly drawn upon our energy as teenagers and the adolescence I had. It's not autobiographical, except for the scene where Diego questions Gael about how he fucked his girlfriend in the hotel. This actually happened to me when I was playing for a football team, and it involved someone who was then a very close friend. It wasn't difficult for me to write this scene, because I already had the dialogue. There are specific things that only very close people would know. For example, our family had a car with the same name as that in the film,[2] and our mother in Mexico City lives in a street after which we named a town in the film.

EMMANUEL LUBEZKI: I was so happy when I read it – because it was so close to us and to our lives. It was a story that we had talked about for many years, mainly while getting drunk in bars while eulogizing our love of road movies. We would talk about this crazy idea of a road movie with two guys and a girl. To then suddenly see all this stuff written down by Alfonso and his brother Carlos was amazing. The film offered portraits of people that we know and captured them so well. I immediately told them that I had to shoot the movie.

GAEL GARCÍA BERNAL *actor*: I think that this film has a real edge to it and also a lot of depth. I also have to say that I think it's the best script I've ever read. I was laughing from the first paragraph, and really enjoying it so much. The characters and the situations were so alive but also full of subtleties. The depth of the film is perhaps surprising, because it really comes from a very clichéd story. I mean, two guys taking a road trip with a woman – how B-movie is that? It's *Porky's* meets *Dude, Where's my Car?* But *Y tu mamá* had a genuine reason to exist and a connection to real kids who were experiencing the loss of innocence.

EMMANUEL LUBEZKI: It was also important, and perhaps not unconnected, that the film was independently financed. One of the reasons that film was slow to evolve in Mexico was that the directors had to wait for the government to fund them. I have to say that through a combination of luck, charm – he is the most charming – and judgement, he met Jorge Vergara. Now Jorge is hooked on movies. I had dinner with him last week and he told me

[2] The car is called Betsabé. In the booklet that accompanies the aforementioned DVD there is a whole chapter devoted to the car and its history.

Y tu mamá también: Alfonso Cuarón (far right) huddles with his actors

he was fucked. I asked him why and he said, 'Because I love making movies so much.'

ALFONSO CUARÓN: In Julio's room there's a poster for *Harold and Maude* (1971). I wanted to put Godard's *Masculin-Féminin* (1966) in because that was the only conscious reference Carlos and I had when writing the script. But it's probably for the best that the poster didn't arrive. Character-wise *Harold and Maude* probably has more to do with my film in terms of the relationship between male and female. It's also a beautiful film.

CARLOS CUARÓN: Alfonso and I wanted to make a very realistic movie that would be like a candid camera. Chilango, generically speaking, is what we use in Mexico City. It's the language that all Chilangos and all Mexicans would understand. What we did, and what is original, is that we used hardcore Chilango, and you rarely see this in movies. You see it more maybe now as it's become slightly standardized. In *Amores Perros* they also speak Chilango but it's not hardcore Chilango. We were the first to do it with that freedom, that freshness if you will, and it played very well.

EMMANUEL LUBEZKI: I love the fact that the style that we found to shoot in really suited the movie. When we started work, we weren't cutting and we were shooting without covering, which is quite a risky thing to do. I remember Alejandro González Iñárritu coming to the set and telling us that we were insane, that we were ruining the rhythm of our movie because we didn't have anywhere to go. Because he's our friend and because we rate his work, we panicked – for one night. Then we watched what we had shot, and decided it was still the way that we were going to do it. And I really think that this was the best way to tell the story.

The entire movie is shot hand-held. This all goes back to our original idea of fifteen years ago, in which we would do a low-budget road movie that would allow us to go with some young actors and semi-improvise scenes and have a bare storyline but not be afraid of adding things as we went. We also wanted to work with a lot less equipment, because we felt that the last two movies we had done together in Hollywood before this one had both had a little bit too much. Everything was so slow because everyone was trying to make their work the best possible and everything was so expensive and there was a crew of something like a hundred and thirty people and this can really rob the project of momentum. This also robs you of the liberty to experiment. By consciously making *Y tu mamá* smaller and by working in *a cappella* fashion we could move faster and really let the actors go.

In its entirety it is the movie that I am most proud of, full-stop. I see other movies that I have shot and I often like moments from them but I have never liked a whole movie, except for this one. I love the story, I love the actors and I love the surroundings.

Gael García Bernal and Diego Luna acted together in El Abuelo y yo *and indeed were friends since early childhood.*

GAEL GARCÍA BERNAL: It almost seemed as if we had spent twenty years in rehearsal for the film . . . Diego and I were twenty when we were doing the film, playing characters who were supposed to be sixteen, so it was fun to make fun of that, but it also contributed to the evolution of our friendship. We became partners in crime, but in a much more serious way. It was great to work with Diego again. I grew up with him and, to use a football metaphor, we played very well together – because when one of us was about to pass the ball, the other instinctively knew where it was going. We were also able to share in each other's goals. Isn't football wonderful to use as a metaphor?

Making the film was incredible, one of the happiest experiences I have had. I would reduce it all to the seven-minute take at the end of the film when the characters are drunkenly talking and dancing in the bar.

© Focus Features

Visions of Light: Emmanuel Lubezki at work on *Y tu mamá también*

Everything was really precise and synchronized, all the crew having at least six tasks to perform, and yet through teamwork and spirit it all came together perfectly. I also think that this scene reveals Alfonso's true qualities as a director. He would arrive at the location and talk through with the actors and block the scene and then think about where to put the camera. It is the good directors who do this. They work around the story, the actors and the life of the film.

I have many favourite scenes. I love the scenes where Tenoch and Julio fight, and I also love all the car scenes where they are talking.

It would have been much easier if the guy I had to kiss weren't my best friend in real life! That was like jumping into cold water. But you just have to go for it. And in terms of my career it was very liberating, because after that I was no longer able to be pigeon-holed. I was able to do what I wanted.

There were obviously instances of men who completely disagreed with it. It must have touched a very raw nerve inside them. On the other hand, the majority really went for it and understood it. I was at screenings where people were clapping. This is another aspect of the *Y tu mamá* experience that I really savoured, seeing how deeply involved people became when watching it. I'm also not specifically referring to Mexico but also abroad, and especially in England where people also shouted and clapped. People became very passionate about it. Which is surprising.

Released in Mexico by Fox, Y tu mamá también *grossed over $9.5 million dollars. In the UK, where it was released by Icon, the film took £1.6 million, and in the US, with* IFC *as its distributor, $13.6 million. The box-office performance was equally impressive throughout Europe and other key territories.*

CARLOS CUARÓN: I was surprised by the success. We have a huge young population in Mexico, and we knew it, but we weren't pre-determined about it. We made the movie we wanted and didn't give a fuck about marketing or how to sell it.

I have my own thermometer when writing, and with this specific script I was laughing a lot, even though it's not a comedy. I had a feeling it was going to work, but perhaps not as well as it did. In the first place, with these things, you can never tell. In the second place, when I work, whether it's with Alfonso or whoever else, I'm not thinking in terms of box office or festivals and awards. I just want to do my thing.

ALFONSO CUARÓN: The film, ultimately, is about themes that are very

Cooling off: Gael García Bernal and Diego Luna in *Y tu mamá también*

Y tu mamá también: Gael García Bernal

universal. It's about the experience of searching for identity: and that breaks boundaries of country, class, sex and race. It's also an on-going process. As Freud remarked, this search for identity doesn't stop until you're dead. Also, happily for me and for the film, we touched a chord with a lot of people. We also saw a reality in Mexico that a lot of people were completely unaware of. But if we had made a documentary then a lot of people wouldn't have cared and consequently wouldn't have seen the film.

The journey that Tenoch and Julio take subtly reveals a lot about the country itself. Voice-over narration (a device sparingly used throughout the film) reveals that a migrant worker is killed in an accident because of a poorly located pedestrian crossing and a fisherman loses his livelihood to the economically lucrative tourism industry.

CARLOS CUARÓN: Those moments were certainly spotted by critics abroad. In Mexico, many of the critics didn't see it, perhaps because it's their reality and for them was nothing new. This is not true for all critics. The reviews were 80 per cent positive; the other 20 per cent totally missed it.

LEONARDO GARCÍA TSAO *critic/academic*: Mine was one of the few negative reviews it got. I think that it is very well made and I think that Alfonso is technically a very skilled film-maker. I also think however that he is very superficial. He is perfect for Hollywood. I thought the narration was a ploy to imbue the film with a false depth.

ALFONSO CUARÓN: I was in Venice when the film opened there – and it went on to win two prizes in the writing and acting categories – and at the press conference a journalist described the film as reactionary and bourgeois and how dare I, in a country filled with many social and economic problems, do a stupid film about some kids who want to get laid. My answer to him was that I thought he was racist. Why is it that they can accept a European film-maker dealing with things in a middle-class or universal context, but Latin Americans are put in a box where we have to make social-realist ideological films? In the 1960s Mexico and Latin America were part of this very ideological movement of film-making; and I think that these overtly political films are so important and it's great that they exist. But it's like saying that Mexican artists have to continue to produce murals because Diego Rivera[3]

[3] Born in Guanajuato in 1886, Rivera is thought the greatest Mexican painter of the twentieth century, credited with the reintroduction of fresco into modern art and architecture, famed also for radical political views and his romance with Frida Kahlo.

was a muralist and so politically aware. My approach and the criticisms the film suffered were also in part due to the fact that, for good or for bad, I have been living outside of Mexico for twelve years now but going all the time back to Mexico so that I can comprehensively follow the social events that are going on.

A lot of the things that I represent in the film have social connotations, but for Carlos and me what was more important was the human dynamic. Part of the point was how oblivious Julio and Tenoch are to the world around them. Yes, they're trying to get laid, and for them their biggest problem turns out to be the fact that they have betrayed each other with their respective girlfriends. But around them an entire culture is being stripped right in front of their eyes.

GUILLERMO ARRIAGA *writer*: I think that *Y tu mamá también* is among my five favourite films of the last five years. I didn't go to the premiere; I paid my money and went to see it in a very small rural Mexican city where the audience was quite macho. You cannot imagine the silence when Gael and Diego kiss. I was absolutely thrilled, and very moved by it. I called Carlos the moment I left the cinema to tell him that I viewed it as a major moment for Mexican cinema in an international sense.

GAEL GARCÍA BERNAL: Well, it certainly doesn't patronize or ridicule its characters; it respects them. This struck a chord all over the world because it was a very universal film despite being set in a specific location with a specific social strata.

There was widespread surprise when the film was rated '18' within Mexico, thus prohibiting a teenage audience – who might perhaps prove most receptive to seeing their loves and the challenges they face presented on screen – from actually seeing it.

CARLOS CUARÓN: The rating thing is very stupid. Alfonso and I were the first to charge the ratings system in Mexico as being illegal because it goes against the freedom of a parent to raise their child. The film was given a certificate that restricted it to only those of eighteen years of age and older. As a responsible parent, I should be allowed to bring my kid. We criticized the fact that the ratings system in Mexico is controlled by the Department of State. We want it to be an autonomous entity, just like the Electoral Institute in Mexico or the Commission of Human Rights in Mexico. Starting from that, we wanted the whole ratings system changed. In the light of all the fuss that we made when our movie was released, the new administration claimed that they reviewed the whole thing when patently they didn't. We are still against the members of the board deciding whether or not I am responsible enough to bring my kid to the movie.

GAEL GARCÍA BERNAL: The decision was shameful. It was, once again, the government depriving Mexican people of respect. It was complete censorship. In other places that we went to, such as Chile, Argentina and Spain, the film was given a less prohibitive certificate, which encouraged parental guidance. The Mexican government never grows tired of ridiculing people. In Mexico there are some laws and restrictions relating to cinema that are almost avant-garde and quite cool, but on the other hand we have these faceless bureaucrats who establish by their own paradigms and parameters what a film is and who it should be seen by.

People have claimed that the controversy generated by the film was beneficial to it but I don't think that's true. Without its restrictive certificate, many more people would have seen it. Mexico is a young country – 50 per cent of the population is under thirty – and so many more young kids would have been able to see the film. Those that did had to break the law to do so, thus creating a really fucked-up double moral standard.

ALFONSO CUARÓN: We sued the ratings board . . .

It's one of the many ways in which the Institutional Revolutionary Party (PRI) was very clever in disguising censorship with civic and democratic masks. There is an organization called RTC – Directorate of Radio, Television, and Cinema – and they are the ones who control the airwaves. There is a case to be made in terms of legislation to prevent the guys from the big corporations from completely taking over, but we are talking about a corrupt country. In terms of censorship, every single film that is released in Mexico has to go through a ratings board. I am all for ratings except this ratings board is controlled by the government, so it is political censorship. The person running this bureau has been the same person for the last twenty years, and so everything depends on the humour and taste of this person. This person feels himself to be a liberal and often overrules his advisers and has made comments such as: 'My colleagues felt this should be an "18" but I think this is an important film so I am giving it a "15".' So whoa! It is this one person who decides.

I am all for ratings, but I also believe in parents being empowered in terms of making decisions as to what their kids can and cannot see. I think it is important to make people responsible but I also believe in freedom and I think that freedom and responsibility are very similar. That was part of our plea; more involvement from parents.

The most important thing is to take the ratings system away from the government, to create a board that is independent of government and of any private group. In this group you would have representation of people made up of different religions, races, political persuasions, etc., and that would be, in my view, a better way to proceed. Obviously the government would be involved but they would not be in control. Our campaign revealed that the ratings system is illegal and that it contravenes a lot of fundamental legal rights in Mexico. The government is responding basically by ignoring us and hoping we will go away, but we still have the legal action in place. The government felt the necessity to show that they were the good guys and created a congress to define new ways of rating but it is typical of the government that I could not attend but Carlos was invited and went and listened to a series of speeches. It felt like a preliminary thing but the next day in the papers it was reported as the sitting of a panel in which people such as Carlos Cuarón supported and agreed with everything that was said. I mean, he was just present; he didn't even open his mouth or anything!

You have the same problem in the UK; I'm thinking of the furore around the language in Ken Loach's *Sweet Sixteen* (2002). Kids speak like this, but if they want to see a film about themselves they have to see one that shows how a censor would like them to speak. Why are they so afraid of kids seeing themselves the way they are? By censoring it you are not going to stop kids speaking like this. By censoring a movie in which kids have sex you are not going to stop them. With *Y tu mamá* there were a lot of parents and sexual educators who were promoting the film to be seen by the parents and by the kids and for them to have conversations about it.

Then the board said it wasn't about the sex, it was about the drugs. We realized that *Almost Famous* (2000) by Cameron Crowe had a much higher use of drugs but that was rated a 'B', the equivalent of a '15'. This is also a Mexican-film and an American-film thing. Their attitude is that you can see Americans using drugs but not Mexicans because, hey, we don't use drugs.

We were also very pissed off with Fox, our distributor, when we began legal proceedings because they made it clear that they didn't want any part of it. It's sad that a country that is supposedly going through democratic change still has an institute in which the same guy is still in power.

LEONARDO GARCÍA TSAO: It pandered. That's why Alfonso and Carlos were so outraged that the film got a restricted rating. It was a publicity ploy to claim that they had been censored. In Mexico anyone can get into the cinema once they have paid for their ticket. There's no real control. The Cuarón brothers are very smart.

© Focus Features

Y tu mamá también: Verdú and Luna

ALFONSO CUARÓN: I consider *Y tu mamá* a cousin to *Amores Perros* and I think that this is true for audiences in Mexico too. For many years in the 'Golden Age' of Mexican cinemas there were melodramas and a romanticized idea of reality, and you would be aware of class difference but it was so romanticized that you would always fall for the idea of the servant marrying the rich guy. This romanticized reality was taken over by the soap operas. And what happens now is that audiences in Mexico want to see something that is very direct and which presents reality as it is. They want to recognize themselves; they don't want a romanticization of their lives. In that sense I think that *Y tu mamá* and *Amores Perros* are cousins, because both deal with a society that is fractured by class.

GUILLERMO DEL TORO: What is wrong in doing *Y tu mamá*, a film described by some Mexican critics as *Beavis and Butthead*, as a sex comedy/road movie in which we recognize our social identity? This film took a proven generic mould and turned it on its head. Where is the sin in that? This is what makes it good.

* * *

Another Mexican success of 2001 saw the return of Guillermo del Toro to Mexico for the purposes of a long-cherished endeavour.

BERTHA NAVARRO *producer*: Guillermo had done *Mimic*, and it was very tough. He tried to make a personal film in impossible circumstances. The end of *Mimic* actually has nothing to do with del Toro, and he was very divided by the compromise. After that experience he wrote many scripts. And several projects, including *The Count of Monte Cristo* with Coppola, fell through. So we felt, 'Why not now make *The Devil's Backbone*?'

GUILLERMO DEL TORO: I had been trying to make the story fit with the Mexican Revolution for many years, and it just wasn't working. For one thing, I realized that the Mexican Revolution has never ended, and secondly it was a very complicated mess with factions being subdivided into other factions. There were a series of intestinal wars in Mexico that didn't stop until the 1930s or later. It was very dirty metaphorically, and I wanted the war to be a war that happened within a family, an intimate war where brothers killed brothers – and that was the Spanish Civil War. I wanted a war movie where you could have the war be geographically far away but also have it created within the walls of the orphanage in a very metaphorical way.

Del Toro's script is set in 1938, with Franco's forces poised to rout the Republicans. Ten-year-old Carlos (Fernando Tielve), son of a fallen Republican, is sent to a remote orphanage run by sympathetic leftists Carmen

Guillermo del Toro and 'kid' on the set of *The Devil's Backbone*

(Marisa Paredes) and Casares (Federico Luppi). But there is much there to unnerve him, from the attentions of bullies to an unexploded bomb in the courtyard; the ominous approach of Franco's troops to the orphanage's walls; teacher Conchita's (Irene Vicido) brooding boyfriend Jacinto (Eduardo Noriega), and the presence of the ghost of a boy called Santi, who ominously predicts, 'Many of you will die . . .'

GUILLERMO DEL TORO: You have Fascism represented by Eduardo Noriega's character Jacinto, and you have the people, represented by the children, and you have the old Republicans represented by Marisa Paredes [Carmen] and Federico Luppi [Casares]. All of them felt they were safe from the effects of the war when they were really re-enacting the war, bit by bit. I felt that the overwhelming image of the movie was the ghost looking at the bomb. It's a movie that doesn't say that everything ends up happily; it says that the bomb never exploded, the ghost never left the place and the only thing you have as a positive is that the children are going to march.

I have a very early drawing that I made when I finished *Cronos* that featured a man drowning in a pool with blood floating from his forehead. It was taken from below and I loved this image. All of a sudden I thought, 'What if a ghost of a guy that has been thrown into a pool with an injury to his head actually walked around with a trail of blood? I found this idea so compelling that I thought this would be the only terrifying thing about the ghost. The rest of it would be like a porcelain doll. It would actually be quite a sad ghost. The idea of showing it very early in the movie was my hope that the movie would eventually clarify for the audience that you shouldn't be afraid of a ghost – you should be afraid of the living. Never fear the dead, fear the living, they are the real danger.

BERTHA NAVARRO: Spain for him was great on *The Devil's Backbone*. It is still a relatively small film in terms of budget but I think that the film would have been difficult to make within Mexico.

Latin American co-production certainly opened up new possibilities for funding. This is especially true of co-productions with Spain; this has been a valuable source of finance. *The Devil's Backbone* was a very special thing. Pedro Almodóvar had seen *Cronos* and met Guillermo at a festival in Miami, and invited Guillermo to come to him if he ever felt that he had a project that could be made in Spain. Many years passed and we called them to say that we do have a project, and they said, 'Great!' They met up again at the Guadalajara Film Festival and the film happened very quickly after that.

GUILLERMO DEL TORO: I had a very happy experience on the film. Film has shown me over the years that you have to remain malleable when faced with financial problems. You have to find the positives under these circumstances. There was a very clear way for me to finance *The Devil's Backbone*, and I had already set it during the Spanish Civil War so I didn't have to make changes as financial considerations as I already was creatively engaged before talking to Pedro and Augustin Almodóvar. I also felt that I would benefit from the international cast and the international *experience*, and I was happy to open myself to it. I learned a lot from working in Europe – I especially loved the fact that they drink wine at their lunch break . . .

IMCINE's approach is very archaic and elitist. It's also a very classicist. It is almost a form of racism. When people ask me why I went to the States I tell them that I would have been perfectly happy to make movies in Mexico for the rest of my life but there was never an open door, you were always, every time, having to kick it open. Even as late as 2000 when we were trying to raise money for *The Devil's Backbone* I went to the head of IMCINE and asked what it was that I was doing wrong. I pointed out that my movies had made a lot of money internationally, had won a lot of prizes internationally and yet you refuse to support me. They said that they didn't think I needed their support. I replied that of course I need it. No. I didn't need it for a project like *Mimic* but this is me trying to do something else. It was a no-win relationship, and has continued like that.

Few people know this but Guillermo Navarro and I were meeting at my home in Austin to discuss the visuals of *The Devil's Backbone* while Guillermo was shooting *Spy Kids* for Robert Rodriguez. I was showing him some Hammer movies and some Mario Bava movies. He literally arrived at the set of *The Devil's Backbone* with only half a day of prep. He shot *Spy Kids* to a Friday, travelled on Saturday, prepped for half a day on Sunday and then began shooting on Monday. But we didn't feel rushed because we know each other so well. After we had tested different kinds of filters for the brown sepia tones, we knew exactly what we were doing from that moment on. Guillermo is one of those brothers that you are not given genetically but that you somehow find through life. We bought our house only because Guillermo lives near by.

The Spirit of the Beehive is a seminal movie for me. I even modelled the girl in *Cronos* exactly on Ana Torrent. That movie, along with the films of Buñuel and the films of Hitchcock, is almost a part of my genetic make-up, buried deep in my DNA. Visually, however, I tried to make *The Devil's Backbone* completely different from other Spanish Civil War movies. They normally texture it in a different way. I wanted to get the dryness of the landscape and the fact that the orphanage seemed to be almost out of a Mervyn Peake novel – a lonely building in a land of nothing.

One of the things that intrigued me about the Spanish Civil War – and indeed something that intrigued me about any war, even as a kid – was, 'Why don't they go away? Why don't they hide in a cave? How can you not see the oppressors coming?' All these little musings are because war is not really a purely geographical occurrence. It really permeates our everyday existence and every act that we do.

The American release of *The Devil's Backbone* was at a very unfortunate time – shortly after the events of September 11th. Seeing the film in a post–September 11th climate made me understand things in the movie that I hadn't understood before. It became more relevant. I also understood that when the worst possible situation occurs, you don't have to be near it – it comes to you.

There are a number of visual references to Alfred Hitchcock and Luis Buñuel in the film: for example, a wooden leg worn by the Marisa Paredes character, and a very Hitchcockian keyhole shot.

Something wicked this way comes: *The Devil's Backbone*

Marisa Paredes as the Buñuellian Carmen in *The Devil's Backbone*

GUILLERMO DEL TORO: Both Hitchcock and Buñuel have great keyhole moments. There is a great one in *El* (1952) that involves a knitting needle ready to poke out somebody's eye. In order to get our shot we made an over-sized keyhole. I used to call it the Hitchcock keyhole because it was like one of the over-sized props that Hitchcock used to get depth of field in films such as *Dial M for Murder* (1953) or the cup of tea that Ingrid Bergman drinks in *Notorious* (1946). It's certainly a Hitchcockian–Buñuelian moment, and I dreamed for so long about this sequence and wanted so much for it to be successful. When I finally made it, I was filled with a childish sense of glee at being a little closer to my bastion of heroes . . .

6
Japón, El crimen del padre Amaro, Nicotina, and *El Misterio del Trinidad*

By the end of 2002 Mexico boasted the fifth-biggest international box office by admissions (154 million) and approximately three thousand screens, the largest number in Latin America. The total box office in Mexico had continued to rise (up by 8.4 per cent on 2001 with receipts of $483 million), as had the increased appetite for locally produced films among Mexican audiences (9 per cent of the total box office in 2002 compared with 8.2 per cent the previous year). In contrast, production levels had dramatically declined. In 2002 only fourteen films were produced within Mexico, down from twenty-one in 2001 and twenty-eight in 2000. Of these films, IMCINE, *the state-backed film institute, produced just four, compared with seven in 2001 and seventeen in 2000.*

ALFREDO JOSKOWICZ *film-maker/Director,* IMCINE: It's a paradoxical situation. Mexican cinema is growing and yet fewer films are being produced annually. But the films have improved immeasurably in terms of the sophistication of their narratives. They are beautifully shot and have skilful acting; their production values and technical details are generally much higher. Also, the films now deal with themes that appeal to Mexican audiences and are attracting younger audiences to the screens, something that has not happened in many years.

ÁNGELES CASTRO *Director,* CCC: Many Mexican films work well and win awards at festivals, but without a huge publicity machine it's very difficult for them to become as widely seen. For example, *Japón* by Carlos Reygadas won many awards and was well received at festivals, but it didn't necessarily do that well when released abroad.

Japón, *released in 2002, concerns a man in his sixties (Alejandro Ferretis) who leaves Mexico City and heads to a remote mountainous region, intending to commit suicide. A group of hunters direct him toward a village overlooking a canyon, whereupon he finds lodging with a pious widow in her eighties by the name of Ascen (Magdalena Flores), whose property is being coveted by a money-grubbing relative. As days go by in this strange environment, the visitor feels his suicidal tendencies recede while he becomes closer to his selfless host.*

ALFONSO CUARÓN *director*: There have been examples of recent Mexican product that has been made with the explicit intention of reaching audiences, and what happens is that the audiences don't give a shit. This is what happens when you try to second guess what audiences want. They're happy to tell you what they want to see, but then you make that movie, you show it to that audience and they're not surprised because they already know it. And it was probably better in their imagination. Audiences may say, 'Oh, I want to see another Bond movie.' They want to see what is already familiar to them. But every so often they also like to be surprised. There are many different kinds of audiences and I would hate that cinema becomes completely subservient to entertainment. A film that I consider one of the most remarkable to come from Mexico in the last thirteen years is *Japón*, and that is not a film that you could call entertainment, but it is an amazing piece of art: the use of sound, space and time is so rare and so strange. In terms of style *Japón* is very different to the films of Alejandro [Iñárritu], Guillermo [del Toro] or myself, and perhaps is more remarkable. I guess it belongs to what Paul Schrader would term a 'transcendental style'. For me, that's the most difficult to do, and I would love to be able to do this. I know that I can deal with expensive special effects but this I would really love to do.

With *Japón* my company tried to get distribution for the film in the States. I am not surprised that it hasn't got distribution because it's not a mainstream film. I relate very much to the work of Carlos Reygadas. People compared the film to Tarkovsky or Kiarostami but it reminded me more of Sokurov. Sokurov is one of my favourite film-makers right now; I also consider him to be one of the most important. For me, the idea of reaching audiences is not paramount; if you do then that's great. It terms of the industry that's a different thing and I think it's important to differentiate industry and cinema. It is also true that the healthier the industry you have, the more possibilities you have to take a shot at cinema.

CARLOS CUARÓN *writer/director*: Carlos Reygadas is doing his own thing, a very low-budget kind of thing, and he really doesn't want to tell a story – he is 'sculpting in time', to borrow from his beloved Tarkovsky.

CARLOS REYGADAS *director*: I was alone in Brussels studying law when I decided I wanted a career in cinema. I started going to the Museum of

© Lisa Roze (Artificial Eye)

Carlos Reygadas

Cinema, and saw perhaps three films a day. I like Roberto Rossellini very much, and the conditions in which he had to shoot with whatever was there. Rossellini was a master at using the world as it is to create everything he needed for his stories. For me, Dreyer is also great. *Ordet* is one of the most moving films I've ever seen in my life, a miracle of film. Bresson is also a master, especially in the way he works with actors and uses sound. *A Man Escaped* [1956] is a personal favourite. Tarkovsky was the one to really open my eyes. When I saw his films I realized that emotion could come directly out of the sound and the image, and not necessarily from the story-telling.

I realized that I had to go to film school to find the human team and the materials, to generally have *access* to things. While I was preparing for the exams I met Diego Martinez Vignatti, an Argentinian director of photography. It was Diego who persuaded me to do a short that I would be able to present as part of my entry credentials, and he also offered to provide me with access to a Super-8 camera and film stock. The next day, I had a storyboard and a completed scenario and had chosen the actors; in fact, everything was prepared. I had so many stories I wanted to tell and so many ideas in my head.

I then completed three further pieces in a similar way. Following that, I made another short film entirely by myself, because I wanted to learn and understand the whole process.

I then began working on the scenario for *Japón*. It was practical and relatively easy to make because it's set in an area I know well, close to Mexico City, and is also the house of my grandparents who live in the area. I worked with the team I had worked with on my shorts and we had to work very hard in an organized manner to make it. I prepared the script and the storyboards and decided that the film would have to be very practical and well prepared and consist of 300 shots. In fact it turned out to be 302 . . .

When I first saw Iranian films some years ago, I was struck by geographical, political and religious similarities, though Islam is perhaps more roughly applied there than Catholicism in Mexico – but socially the presence of religion is very similar. I was impressed by the work of Abbas Kiarostami and his decision to use very long takes with few cuts. I also appreciated that there was, in fact, lots happening within the scenes and within the little details. It's such details that I'm interested in. I'm not interested in the operations of MI5.

The lead actor in *Japón*, Alejandro Ferretis[1] is actually a friend of my parents, and has been for a very long time. I've known him since I was a very little boy, and he always appeared as special to me. He lived through the sixties in a very combative way; he reads voraciously and has a tremendous gift for languages. He was always asking me complex, stimulating questions,

[1] Ferretis committed suicide in March 2005.

often from a Marxist perspective, which we would then endlessly debate and discuss. So when I was writing the script I was always thinking of him, especially as he had often expressed his admiration for Arthur Koestler.[2] When we actually started shooting he started to glamorize himself a little bit, as if he thought we were shooting a French perfume ad. However, he soon learned that I didn't want any of that and that I actually wanted him to do very little, which reminds me again of my earlier point about Bresson. Alejandro had never acted before.

Magdalena Flores, who plays Ascen, had never acted either. In fact all the cast are non-actors. I wanted to work with pure, real matter, largely for the sake of authenticity. I can't imagine any actress in the world performing the role of Magdalena. This sense of authenticity was especially important for the sexual scene, in which Magdalena is really afraid and really modest but at the time has so great a sense of honour that she has to fulfil the promise that she made. This very real intellectual and spiritual fight she is having would have been impossible for an actress.

I did speak to professional actors, and most I met were sick with narcissism. One actress said that she would have done the nude scenes when she was younger but that an audience would vomit if they saw her naked now. I actually saw around three hundred women for the part, and there was always something more powerful about the peasant women I auditioned for the role. Magdalena was unaware of the fact that she wasn't beautiful because she is unaware of popular conceptions of beauty. It was an ethical and cultural problem concerning her nudity, which was overcome by mutual trust.

I had actually found another woman to play the part of Ascen and worked very closely with her, but one week into shooting she simply vanished, leaving a note saying that she had broken her hips. In Mexico this simply means that she was afraid so I didn't try to look for her in any hospital. We found Magdalena when we were shooting the slaughter of the pig as she had come to buy some meat and, of course, she initially said 'No' when approached about the part but finally consented after we went to see her family and developed the relationship naturally. Magdalena Flores is a very intelligent woman and did beautiful work. She didn't even have a script; she simply took direction on a scene-by-scene basis.

Shooting the sex scene was zero traumatic, and very simple. It's a bit like

[2] Koestler was a journalist who fought in the Spanish Civil War, renounced Communism after Stalin's show trials, and wrote *Darkness at Noon* (1941), about an ageing Bolshevik awaiting execution.

© Artificial Eye

Alejandro Ferretis in *Japón*

© Artificial Eye

Death is all around: *Japón*

virginity. Girls are told about sex and what is going to happen for years, then when it happens they think, 'All that shit for *this*?' Given Alejandro's liberal sensibilities I anticipated that he would have no problem with the scene, but as it often happens in life, at the hour of truth it was maybe harder for the man than for the woman. For Magdalena she had nightmares beforehand, but when the day came it was a very small, intimate crew and after some tequila she was very tranquil. I also kept the directions very simple to both Magdalena and Alejandro. And it was much like in the film; Alejandro was supposed to be in control but became more hesitant as he became nervous.

I showed the finished film to the people in the village but unfortunately I had to cut the sex scene because I was worried that Magdalena might suffer abuse and teasing; there is a saying, 'Little town, big hell.' You know, Mexico is a very special place; some of the population is Western and some of them are not. In terms of the cast, the only one with Western sensibilities was Alejandro so it's hard to really gauge what they feel and how they react. I know that they really laughed at the scene involving the screaming of the pig – in fact, anything involving animals prompted laughter, which is certainly not the reaction you will get in the UK. It's not even the reaction you might get in more highly populated cities in Mexico.

To me, titles are a necessary evil – ideally they wouldn't exist. Paintings, for example, don't always have titles. I wanted to do the same with my film and leave it untitled. I then thought about calling it 'Untitled' but that would just be pretentious. And we have to give it a name so that people can refer to it. I should have just called the film 'Magdalena and Alejandro in the Canyon' or 'Love at Last Sight' or something like that . . . I always wait until the end to find a title, so I wondered, 'What is this film about, after all?' For me it is partly about the cycle of light coming again after night. I was struck therefore by the notion of the sun rising which of course has connotations with Japan. I could have called it 'Korea' or 'Taiwan' but these countries are more closely associated with microchip technology. People also often associate other characteristics with Japan such as haiku poetry, a respect for the elderly and the repression of feelings. There is also the culture of the Samurai and in many ways Alejandro represents this with his veneer of toughness and the impression he gives that he is totally in control. Of course, all he really wants is to cry with his mother holding him. This is perhaps what most of us men really want.

There are also contradictory ideas in the film. People have interpreted Ascen's act differently. Some believe that she does what she does because there is a force that compels her to save him; other people believe that she does it because of ideas relating to Christian sacrifice. There are also those that interpret Ascen as simply realizing what may perhaps be her last opportunity to enjoy physical pleasure. All those things are and can be there.

Japón was shot on ordinary 16 mm, but in front of the primary lens a special anamorphic lens was introduced, so that the actual frame is a standard 1:37 ratio but the images are squeezed. The blow-up to 35 mm was a standard blow-up by photographical process. There are few 16 mm 'scope films, but it's actually quite a simple process that gives a very grainy look, which I like. I actually got the contact for the process after watching Gaspar

Noé's *I Stand Alone* (1998).[3] I had already decided that the film had to be in Cinemascope but if I hadn't shot it in the way I did, then I would have had to do it on 35 mm Panavision film and equipment which is both expensive and heavy.

Diego Martinez Vignatti has a very, very strong character and he understands films in the same way that I do. He also believes, pretentious though it may sound, that art is individual expression and so, prior to shooting, we talked at length about how the film was going to look in terms of the colour, the contrast and the texture. The framing we didn't talk about so much, because that is something I do completely by myself – for me framing is so basic and so important. Diego does make some very good suggestions but he also understands that suggestions are just suggestions and that they can be accepted or not accepted.

The music for the final shot revealing the tragedy is by Arvo Pärt[4] and it's an amazing piece of music. That piece of music in fact influenced very much the ending of the film and suggested the images and gave me the key and the clue regarding how to shoot the last shot. The sound in general is also very important and I sometimes believe that sound design is almost half of cinema, especially in terms of expression. Sound can be objective or subjective. I would say that Tarkovsky is a master of subjective sound and Kiarostami is a master of objective sound; I try to use both.

Each one of us chooses our own life. You are not 'more Mexican' as a filmmaker if you stay in Mexico and you are not a traitor if you create products in Iceland, for example. The only question is whether you're interested in product or in personal expression.

Hollywood probably wouldn't invite me but people don't believe me when I say that if they did I wouldn't want to go. That said, I don't want to say no to anything in life but really it's not my goal to shoot my next film with Tom Cruise. If I was in it for the money I should probably be doing another job. I love so much the images and the sounds that I have in my head. That's the reason I do it, no other.

* * *

[3] Photographed by Dominique Colin, Noé's *I Stand Alone* (*Seul contre tous*) has a bleached, grainy look that serves dramatically to heighten its intensity.

[4] Pärt was born in Paide, Estonia, and is a graduate of the Tallinn Conservatory. His significant early works include *Nekrolog*, Symphonie No. 1, Symphonie No. 2 and *Collage über BACH*. In 1968 Pärt's *Credo* was banned, leading him to undertake the first of what would become several periods of contemplative silence. Three 1977 pieces (*Fratres*, *Cantus In Memoriam Benjamin Britten* and *Tabula Rasa*) remain among his most highly regarded.

In 2002 Carlos Carrera released his fourth and most successful feature, El crimen del padre Amaro, *adapted and updated from the novel by Eça de Queiros. It concerns a recently ordained twenty-four-year-old priest (played by Gael García Bernal) who is sent to a small parish church to assist an ageing senior, Benito (Sancho Gracia). But Amaro is then challenged by his attraction to sixteen-year-old Amelia (Ana Claudia Talancón), whose mother has long since been dallying with Benito. And Amaro fast learns that the clerical life offers other temptations, once he has understood how deeply Benito is indebted to a local drug baron.*

Amid the success of privately funded films such as Amores Perros *and* Y tu mamá, El crimen *retained a much closer association with both* IMCINE *and the heritage of Mexican cinema. Actor Pedro Armendáriz – the son of one of Mexico's best-loved 'classic'-era stars – appeared in the picture. And the founder of the production company, Alameda Films, which oversaw the film is producer Daniel Birman, part of a formidable Ripstein dynasty: son of Arturo Ripstein, and grandson of legendary producer Alfredo Ripstein, a cornerstone of the Mexican film industry since 1946.*

© Daniel Birman

A film-making dynasty: Daniel Birman (left) and his grandfather Alfredo Ripstein

DANIEL BIRMAN *producer*: I started studying law, but after two years I left the university to join my grandfather's company in 1991. I started there really knowing nothing – in fact, I didn't even get paid for a long time. But then my grandfather really became interested in my knowing more about the business, how he made films, and taking that experience, and adapting it to newer and more innovative techniques. He has also taught me that you never really finish learning – that there will always be new processes and situations to which you must adapt.

My role in the film actually came twenty-three years after it was initially conceived as a project. Alfredo Ripstein tried to do *El crimen* in 1970 but circumstances intervened. In 1995, after we shot *El Callejón de los milagros* (*Midaq Alley*), we decided it was time to do the film, and we called Carlos Carrera on board. It took us around six or seven years to get the funding, because nobody believed in the project. IMCINE was attached to it only at the very end.

Laura Imperiale is Argentinian by birth, but left the country in 1976. Initially interested in sound, she arrived in Brazil and found work as as an editing assistant for a commercials company. She reached Mexico in 1979, and starting producing documentaries for TV.

LAURA IMPERIALE *producer*: I met Arturo Ripstein and Paz Alicia at the Havana Festival in 1996. I think we made a good impression on each other straight away, but I only found out for sure the following year when I got a call from Arturo inviting me to work on the project he was preparing: *El Evangelio de las maravillas* (*Divine*, 1998). At that time I was working at Producciónes Amaranta with Jorge Sánchez. I suggested involving Jorge to Arturo. We then agreed to produce *El Evangelio* at Amaranta. After that, Jorge and I worked together on four of Arturo's films: *Divine*, *El Coronel no tiene quien le escriba* (*No One Writes to the Colonel*, 1999), *Así es la vida* (*Such is Life*, 2000) and *La perdición de los hombres* (*The Ruination of Men*, 2000). That period of work with Arturo and Jorge was my baptism of fire. On the one hand all the films were co-productions – Brazil, Argentina, Spain, France – on the other, although working with a director as experienced as Arturo presented certain demands, it was also a great apprenticeship. I was slightly apprehensive at first, given that Arturo had a reputation of being a tough person to work with, but I never had a cause for complaint. With Arturo we also made Mexico's first commercially released digital film, *Así es la vida*.

With *El crimen*, Daniel Birman and Alfredo Ripstein invited me to work with them because the project was to be made as a co-production with Spain and with support from Fondo Sur: they had no experience in either of these two areas – and I knew the Spanish co-producer, José María Morales of Wanda Vision, very well, having previously worked with him on several of Arturo's films. Part of my contribution to the production of *El crimen* was Cinecolor, an Argentinian company that was starting to work in Mexico too. What really made me excited about the project, though, was working with Carlos. Despite knowing each other well, we had never had an opportunity to work together.

CARLOS CARRERA *director*: There was also money from a French fund, Artcam, and an Argentinian laboratory, Videocolor. Co-production is an important new avenue. There is, however, also something about co-productions that I don't like at all. You make decisions depending on the co-production. For example you must hire a Spanish or Argentinian actor and adapt the script to fit. There are compromises that you have to make. As a director I am prepared to make them but I don't necessarily have to like them.

I like both rural and urban dramas. *Sin Remitente* (*No Return Address*) takes place in Mexico City. There is a problem in Mexico in that almost all the cultural life takes place in Mexico City. I grew up in Mexico City and I have spent almost all my life here, but my parents are from other places and my grandmother used to always tell me fascinating stories about the places they came from. There are many very other interesting stories to be told. We are a hundred million Mexicans, it's important to reflect our diversity.

The dramatic premise of impossible love almost always works, but I wasn't so interested in the forbidden love between a priest and a young girl. I was more interested in other aspects suggested by the novel: corruption, moral doubt and ethics. I felt there were lots of similarities with the behaviour of the priests in the novel and the priests of our days. There are many places where you can find human beings who as human beings make mistakes; they are as fallible as anyone. There are only two or three films that talk about the church in Mexico and almost 85 or 90 per cent of Mexican people are Catholic so I felt that it was very important to talk about what is going on in the Church. Most people are aware of the relationship between priests and drug dealers and crime lords. The Catholic Church is more of a political institution than it is a spiritual or religious one. Obviously I'm not saying that all priests are corrupt. This is the story of just one character. But we can easily find many more like him throughout our land.

Gael was making Y *tu mamá también* when he was cast. It took us four years to secure the financing to make *El crimen* so he had read the script some time before he became such a big star.

GAEL GARCÍA BERNAL *actor*: Carlos gave me the script and I really liked the idea of exploring the character of this priest who is riddled with moral complexities: someone who places the fear of God above anything else, and yet his personal ambitions and goals compromise this fear. It was great to investigate these themes and this type of story, especially in light of the American scripts that came my way and the parts that I was continually being offered after *Amores Perros*. These parts were all very stereotypical Latin lover types or the troubled boy from the *barrio*.

Like *Amores Perros* it felt absolutely necessary, but the decision to make it was perhaps less instinctive and more conscious and objective. Carlos's style is very different from either Alejandro [Iñárritu]'s or Alfonso [Cuarón]'s and this was also appealing. Having made a lot of films within Mexico I was also intrigued to see what Carlos would come up with next. The working atmosphere was also very different, more traditional if you like, but the film and its themes are very prescient.

CARLOS CARRERA: I tried to decide how to shoot the film in terms of the best way to tell the story and to communicate the central themes. Overall, I

Love in bad faith: Gael García Bernal and Ana Claudia Talancón in *El crimen del padre Amaro*

would describe my style as very classic and, if you like, conventional. It is certainly more conventional than *Amores Perros*.

The violence I didn't want to focus on, but rather indicate that it is simply part of daily life. I think that the focus in this film should be more on the conflict between and within the characters, rather than showing the violence in our society. Mexico is a violent country with a violent culture and violence is a sad fact of everyday life.

Funded and fully supported by IMCINE, *released on an unprecedented 365 screens across Mexico on 8 August 2002 by Columbia Tri-Star,* El crimen del padre Amaro *earned 31 million pesos (approximately $2.8 million/£2 million) on its opening weekend. It has since gone on to gross over $15 million. This attendance ensured that the film, made on a budget of just 20 million pesos (£1.3 million) turned an immediate profit. It was released in the UK under its English-language title,* The Crime of Father Amaro, *by Columbia Tristar on 20 June 2003. Though largely well received, the film failed to attract large audiences and did not have the same controversial impact as it did in Mexico.*

LEONARDO GARCÍA TSAO *critic/academic*: I think that the film is very important in contradicting moral attitudes and the extreme-right Catholic thinking that has so far prevailed during the Vicente Fox regime. It was also important that it was shown with relatively little interference. Yes, there were protests but nobody tried actively to stop it from being exhibited. There was a huge coup, which in effect translated to massive publicity for free. The film was in all the papers and all the extreme-right groups took full-page ads in the papers urging people not to see the film but the ads had the exact opposite effect.

Carlos Carrera is a director who I rate very highly. He's much more academic and perhaps less risky as a film-maker, but I think he has an impressive way of capturing Mexican reality.

The middle classes were extremely attracted to a film that was critical of the Catholic Church. Working-class people in Mexico don't go to the cinema any more. It is too expensive. Each ticket costs on average $4, so if you go with someone that is $8. The working class waits for the pirate video.

GAEL GARCÍA BERNAL: I think that the controversy was expected. We didn't know how intense it would be but we did know that there would be repercussions relating to freedom of speech. The media actually defended the film a lot, pushing the spokespeople from right-wing Catholic groups to make really idiotic, ridiculous pronouncements. The media helped drive public opinion towards supporting the film. As a result, people that may have had no intention of seeing the film went to see it just to fuck these extremist groups over. In Mexico, whenever you are told not to do something, the immediate reaction is to do it.

DANIEL BIRMAN: The controversy that hit *El crimen* evolved in the manner of most speculation: nobody had seen it, and yet everybody was talking about it. Fortunately, alongside the speculation we also had a wonderful film that kept cinemas packed for months. Controversy might have made people attend initially but quality kept them coming back.

CARLOS CUARÓN: The huge success was in part due to the subject. It was also greatly helped by the Catholic Church trying to ban it. They were unable to do this because Mexican society has changed so much. Another huge factor of course is Gael, who's extremely popular. In formal terms *El crimen* is much more like the films of the 1970s, particularly early Ripstein. It was the combination of scandal, Mexican society and the Catholic Church and Gael. It tells you the story in a very linear fashion from A to Z and sometimes people like this.

BERTHA NAVARRO *producer*: It *is* very traditional. I think, when considering the success of the film and the fact that it did not correspond to the style of films like *Amores Perros*, one must factor in the presence of Gael García Bernal. He is a huge figure in Mexico. Box office in Mexico has nothing to do with directors: the Mexican public don't really know who the director is on a particular film. Well, some more knowledgeable ones do, but it's certainly not a key factor, even though in promotion and marketing you always say, 'A film by . . .' Names of directors can sometimes ring a bell but actors are more important. The phenomenon of Gael is beyond importance; he is a huge success.

Secondly, Mexico is a very Catholic country, but the public in Mexico does not like being told what to do. Once the Church and the state told them not to go and see the movie, of course the public was going to do exactly the opposite.

CARLOS CARRERA: I thought that in these times, with this new government, it would be harder to find a strong reaction against the movie. I thought, incorrectly, that we were living in more liberal times.

What saddens me most is that, because of these very conservative groups, the whole world got the wrong idea of what Mexico is. I think that Mexico is the healthy reaction of the audiences that went to see the movie, not the hysterical reaction of these very conservative groups. Mexico appeared as a medieval and regressive country.

I was very amazed and surprised by the film's success. I certainly don't care about money but obviously I like my films to be seen. I like to tell my stories in a comprehensive language for everyone. I am aware at all times of the audience and I like my films to be liked by them.

* * *

Unfolding in 'real time', Nicotina *is a highly stylized black comedy of coincidence about a techie geek, Lolo (Diego Luna), who accidentally gives the wrong computer disk to some Russian gangsters. As a result, the lives of nine highly diverse Mexico City inhabitants entwine in one tumultous night over the whereabouts of a small fortune in diamonds. Released with a sizeable publicity and advertising campaign, the film arguably attempted to marry sophisticated story-telling, high production values and an undoubted star in Diego Luna to seize the moment and capture the renewed hunger for locally produced movies from Mexican audiences.*

MARTHA SOSA *producer*: I think it's dangerous to attempt simply to repeat a formula. *Nicotina* for me has a very different approach both visually and

Diego Luna in the urban black comedy *Nicotina*

thematically. I believe that *Amores Perros* left many people seeking a relief from drama.

I also believe – and this is the reason I joined forces with Laura Imperiale to do it – that at this moment we really need this film. I always try to position myself in the place of the spectator and as a spectator I needed a little light refreshment. Yes, let's talk about reality and how and who we are but let's also not forget to laugh.

HUGO RODRÍGUEZ *director*: I met Martín Salinas when I arrived in Mexico City in 1981. He was a cartoonist and the director of an animation company called CineSur, where I started working, colouring in his drawing and doing some camera animation. In fact, it's largely thanks to him that I'm working in films today. Around that time I also met Laura Imperiale, who already knew Martín. So we've been friends for a long time now, but until then we had never worked together. It was Laura who, after many years of trying, managed to bring us together. For several years I had been trying unsuccessfully to get various projects off the ground, when Laura set about finding a script for me to direct. She made several attempts; she even bought some rights, but the projects didn't bear fruit and we couldn't get them going. On one of Martín's visits to Mexico – I think it was in August 2001 – Laura suggested that he write a script for me to direct. Martín mentioned he had three separate stories that he thought could be combined to make a full-length film. He went back to Argentina and e-mailed them to me, with a suggestion about how they could be joined together. Each in his own country, we started work and, within four months, we already had a presentable script.

MARTÍN SALINAS *screenwriter*: I had been writing fifteen one-hour scripts for a TV series in Argentina, ruled mainly by a production and genre premise: three-to-five characters at the most, one single location; it all had to happen in real time, with as much suspense as possible, and completely different casts and stories each time. The opposite to what happens with 'development hell' – every script I delivered got made, and the series was very successful in terms of rating and reviews, and lasted three seasons. *Nicotina* was born out of that experience. At the very beginning, it was made of these three different independent stories which dealt with the opposite to what you would call 'love stories'. The title I chose for the first version of that three-stories script doesn't translate well into English: *Desamores*.

Those three stories – Lolo and his neighbour Andrea, the pharmacists, and the hairdressers – were written at very different moments. The common denominator, besides the 'No love!' aspect was the conflict between our efforts to try to consciously take control of our lives and make decisions, and chance, misfortune, luck and coincidences, and also our silly attempts to control other people's lives and feelings. I wrote the pharmacists' storyline right after trying to help my wife figure out what was wrong with our bank balance. I guess I became quite mean in pointing out her mistakes. She said she would undoubtedly make more mistakes if I stood there waiting for her to make more mistakes . . . It got worse and worse . . . The hairdressers' story was inspired by real people I know who are not hairdressers, and would probably not end up like Carmen and Goyo if something like that happened to them. But you need only to open the crime section of any newspaper to realize that it is a plausible story.

Hugo read the stories and proposed that we try to find a way to connect them through these two gangsters who break into the pharmacy, while incorporating the diamonds aspect of the story. I tried it and it worked. Then we realized that the cigarettes that were mentioned in one of the stories were closely related to this conflict between cause and effect and the coincidences that I mentioned before. I'm not a smoker. But my wife is . . .

LAURA IMPERIALE: From the moment we read Martín's proposal, we decided that this was the project we would make together. We exchanged ideas by e-mail until we had defined very precisely what the film was about, then Martín started work on the script, and he produced a first draft very quickly. From the outset we saw *Nicotina* as a project that belonged to the three of us, so our working relationship was always marked along those lines. Just over a year after our initial discussions, we were filming. Later on, Martha Sosa joined the original team on the production side. Yes, it really was a team effort, with each member committed to making the best film possible.

Nicotina *is a co-production between Mexico and Argentina. Such productions between Latin American and Spanish-speaking countries have become increasingly necessary in order for these films to make it to the production stage.*

LAURA IMPERIALE: All official co-productions – those made within the framework of agreements signed between governments – receive the nationality of the countries involved; on the basis of which, producers are then entitled to the benefits afforded them by the cinema laws of their respective countries. Tax incentives for the production, the distribution, etc. . . . These agreements oblige you to comply with certain requirements such as having actors from both countries in lead roles, a minimum percentage of private investment, and the participation of heads of production from both countries. The last two points don't create any great difficulties, but the first is always the most difficult and is the one you have to consider very carefully.

Some stories lend themselves to the inclusion of characters from different backgrounds, but many don't. In the case of *Nicotina* we thought the inclusion of Argentinian characters did the story no harm and could even benefit it with the play on the different ways we speak.

Right now in Mexico City we all know someone who is Argentinian – a neighbour, a boyfriend, a colleague, a friend. It's completely believable. It's well known how much Latin Americans have moved throughout the world in recent years. In terms of finance, the money from a co-production is not fundamental but it does help to tie up the financing. Once you have a co-production you can also apply to other funds such as the Programa Ibermedia.

As well as this, it ensures that your film will be shown in cinemas and on television in the country of your co-producer. Despite the fact that at the present time our films don't do very well in the other countries of our region, we are gradually getting the public used to offerings that are not only American. Once they've seen a film they like, the next time they'll try another. I think it helps to grow the market. I think that although the co-production route is not the only one, it is a good method for continuing to produce in the future.

The film plays out largely in real time. A difficult conceit to achieve on screen.

MARTÍN SALINAS: Contrary to what I used to believe, I've found that real time can sometimes make it a lot easier than when you have the freedom to cut to several hours, days or months later. It can even help you have more time within certain scenes when you think of showing characters at a closer range. It does also help a lot when it comes up to building suspense. But, above all, it seems to be a matter of scale. When we first see Carmen, the barber's wife, she's already very angry with her husband. If the Russian guy had not shown up, nothing would have changed; she would have continued feeling angry day after day. But the arrival of the Russian gangster breaks this routine and ends up throwing Carmen and Goyo into a pressure-cooker dynamic in which real time is probably the best possible way to go. Decisions have to be taken right away; it is right now or never. Which is why she makes the first big mistake and gets obsessed with the wrong belly. Same thing with Clara, the pharmacist, or Lolo, the hacker. I think real time is what helps us follow their conflicts and urges us to take certain decisions, second after second. Real time is probably the trick that actually makes these crazy improbable stories look plausible.

HUGO RODRÍGUEZ: The people for whom it was more laborious were the actors. They had to maintain throughout a whole week the emotional continuity of a scene, which, on screen, lasts ten minutes. The nuances of their acting, they had to sustain for a whole day. In film, more than in any other dramatic art, the actor has to have full control over his emotional memory so as to carry forward the continuity of his character, especially as in general a film is not shot chronologically. What happens with a story that takes place in real time is that the acting is condensed. The character is introduced, externalizes his conflict, achieves catharsis, and reaches resolution in a shorter period of time. That was a challenge that I think we resolved well.

A black comedy, Nicotina *also concentrates on numerous social malaises, such as greed, jealousy and the corrupting nature of power and the dangers of increased technology.*

MARTÍN SALINAS: Someone told me that at certain moments *Nicotina* seemed to have been written by an enthusiastic pessimist. I don't think that's my case, but it is true that I enjoy telling funny stories that reveal the darkest side of human nature. Not out of pure nihilism. I just don't think that the world can be simply divided between good guys and bad guys or between good and evil. I find it very appealing to tell a story in which you suddenly find yourself identifying, even for a few seconds, with someone who eventually does something awful. The fact that the audience laughs louder when the film reaches the darkest peaks tells me that what they're watching sounds disturbingly familiar to them. How far would I go, if I knew that if I don't grab those twenty diamonds without actually hurting anybody, some corrupt cop would? I think comedy has this potential to catch people off guard.

When you live in a big city in which little kids beg on the streets for food, like they do in Buenos Aires, and you don't close your eyes to this, your angle on what is unpleasant or not is affected by this. The day I decided to take the script of *Nicotina* to the Sundance/Toscano Screenwriters' Lab for feedback, Argentina was on fire. Middle-class people marched on the streets banging pots and pans in fury because banks had closed their doors to them and their lifetime savings had just been practically confiscated. Thousands of unemployed people were breaking into supermarkets and food shops to grab whatever they could find in order to feed their children. Barbershops were losing their clients, as people would just cut their hair at home. And I remember thinking that there were probably hundreds of desperate Carmen-like men and women out there, ready to dig twenty diamonds in a dead Russian's guts if they had the chance, without batting an eyelid.

One day I called Laura and told her I had a name to suggest for our new production company: Cacerola Films.[5] Laura and Hugo, who were both also born in Buenos Aires, liked it right away.

Latin American readers of the script at the Screenwriters' Lab felt a woman like the barbershop wife was a somewhat familiar real-life type. The same thing with the cop who smuggles cigarettes into the pharmacy; they are a part of the local landscape. In fact, if you have two cops in a Latin American film, and you don't see some sort of crooked corrupt detail in at least one of them, your friends will point it out to you. Over here you think twice before calling the police if you're in trouble. In terms of tone and genre, our goal with *Nicotina* was to try to get people to laugh at things that ring true to them. And for this you need somehow to exaggerate certain cultural and idiosyncratic patterns. In Latin America this seems to lead you very easily to writing black comedy, if not blatant farce. I actually see this as the most challenging aspect of trying to write and produce comedy for the big screen in Latin America.

MARTÍN SALINAS: The Lolo in the draft we gave to Martha Sosa was a plump fat guy in his early thirties. So when they sent the script to Diego for the first time, Hugo wanted him to play Nene. I can't recall what the steps were, as I was in Argentina, but I think it was Martha who proposed to make Lolo younger so that Diego could play it. Diego, who totally belongs to the acting species, loved the idea of playing a character against type like that. I got worried. How could someone so charming and seductive play the character that I had in mind? The timid, plump guy in his early thirties was someone who (according to me) you could feel pity for and even like him despite what he does to his neighbour. The moment I joined Diego and Hugo for a reading, I had the answer.

Nicotina *utilizes the full lexicon of film language, playing with film speed, character point of view and using audacious camera movement.*

HUGO RODRÍGUEZ: Camera movements are a well-established part of film language. As always, the important thing to know is what it is we're telling

[5] *Cacerola* translates as 'pots and pans'.

and how we want to tell it. In the case of *Nicotina*, the decision to use camera movements was a conceptual one. *Nicotina* is a black comedy. A comedy because the characters upset their world in order to get what they want, and a *black* comedy because in the course of upsetting their world and in resolving their desires, violence and death come into play.

The themes we deal with are strong: voyeurism, family violence, exaggerated ambitions. In order for the spectator to reach catharsis, we decided to treat the whole story in a realistic fashion. The intention was (and I think we achieved it) for the audience to be able to relate to parts of the characters' lives – probably not to all of a life, but, yes, to some of each character's minor neuroses.

This had a direct impact on the tone of the acting, the lighting, the set design, the make-up and the wardrobe. I could feel that the realism worked. But . . . Although I knew we'd manage to get the audience to identify with the characters, I was worried that, as the story progressed, we'd gradually lose the potential for catharsis, so that by the time we reached the outburst of violence we wouldn't provoke laughter, because the density of the narrative wouldn't allow it. I didn't want to get to the point where a spectator was hesitant about laughing – I wanted him to laugh first, and then to ask himself what he was laughing about. In this sense, the camera movements allowed me to lighten the narrative. To wink at the spectator. To act as a reminder that there was a narrator and that, after all, we were telling a story.

I think these factors partly explain why we have a film that is popular with younger audiences, although I think what we succeeded in reaching was a good intelligent audience.

With regard to the genre and the tone of the acting, my point of reference was Joel Coen. He's a director who really knows how to use the various dramatic genres and so can distort them effectively. He moves with complete ease from tragedy to comedy (*Fargo*, 1995), from farce to melodrama (*Raising Arizona*, 1987) or from comedy to melodrama (*The Big Lebowski*, 1998). Similarly, he keeps the tone of the acting flirting from one genre to another; in general, he's playing with realism and farce. Strictly speaking, I used more TV references than film references: the formal resolution of series such as *CSI* (*Crime Scene Investigation*), *Witchblade*, or *24*, together with the narrative style of Japanese cartoons like *Cowboy Bebop*, *Eat-man*, and *Aeon*.[6]

[6] *Cowboy Bebop* (*Tengoku no tobira*) was directed by Shinichirô Watanabe and Hiroyuki Okiura. The *Eat-Man* series was directed by Toshifumi Kawase. The *Aeon Flux* series was created by Peter Chung.

I'm interested in human weaknesses. Day by day, it's becoming easier to live in isolation. Our generation feels nostalgia for streets where you could stroll, for markets and small stores; our children are going to miss the malls because, after all, they're a place where you can socialize; and, in a few more years, it's very probable you'll be able to do everything without ever having to leave your home. Lolo is an expression of that situation, a young man who's in control of the virtual world but who is incapable of showing the girl in the next apartment the feelings he has for her. When he does, it's already too late.

But each one of the characters has a dark side. And that's what makes them real, accessible and, in part, likeable.

From the outset, given the people involved in the production (and the Mexican industry was quick to dub the film as being from the same stable as Amores Perros*), the pressure to achieve commercial success was relatively intense.*

MARTÍN SALINAS: From the script onwards, people were very favourable about the project, but it wasn't until the film was finished that expectations about doing well at the box office were raised. I'd meet friends and colleagues and the jokes and comments suggested that there was a chance the film could be a success. But this was when the creative process had already been completed and we were at the stage of launching the film.

Although there are people around who are mean-spirited, in general those of us who work in films in Mexico always want Mexican films to do well. That may sound very romantic, but actually it's very practical. We face a constant struggle against Hollywood, which monopolizes most of the box office. If a domestic film does well, it paves the way for people to go back to watching Mexican cinema. If not, and a couple of years go by without a domestic film being a box-office hit, everything becomes more difficult, from obtaining advertising space that helps to bring audiences into the cinemas to getting the financing for another project.

LAURA IMPERIALE: Although we may not have had the impact of *Amores Perros* and *Y tu mamá también*, *Nicotina* has done well internationally.[7] We see it as a success.

* * *

[7] *Nicotina* was released by Videocine on 230 prints, grossing $4.1 million.

LEONARDO GARCÍA TSAO: For me, one of the most under-estimated Mexican directors is José Luis García Agraz. He is being very under-used and should be making many more films. He makes only personal films; he's not a director for hire, and that can act as a limitation on him. *El Misterio del Trinidad*, his most recent film, I admire – but other people don't seem to be so interested in it. It's a family melodrama – a genre not in vogue, and it has none of the modern kicks. It is linear; it doesn't jump from one character to another and doesn't feature rock songs on its soundtrack. It is very traditional but still very well made and I hope it finds an audience.

The protagonist of Agraz's film is Juan (Eduardo Palomo), illegitimate son of Joaquin, an elderly engineer who spent his life obsessively diving in the waters of the Gulf of Mexico, searching for a sunken seventeenth-century Spanish galleon, the Santísima Trinidad. *On Joaquin's death, Juan (divorced and with a ten-year-old daughter, Ana, of whom he sees little) receives the title to the old man's boat, the* Meridiano, *in his will. However Joaquin's legal heirs did not know of Juan's existence and moreover desire the boat for themselves. Only Juan's half-sister Isabel, herself unhappily married, is sympathetic to Juan. But before the clan can lay hands on Juan, he sets off to find the galleon for himself. At his ex-wife's insistence, however, he is accompanied by Ana.*

JOSÉ LUIS GARCÍA AGRAZ *director*: When I finished *Desiertos mares* (*Desert Seas*, 1995) and bearing in mind the ambiguity of the character of the father at the end of that film, I felt the need to go more deeply into a father character in my *next* film; that's when I began to write the script. The figure of the father has a dominant place in many cultures, and in Mexico it's perhaps the touchstone through which we relate to the world – a paternalistic culture in which it is the father who loves and punishes, gives and takes; only the attainment of maturity will enable us to live in a world without fathers and in which we ourselves are masters of our own destinies.

It was a long and complicated process: I attended the Sundance Screenwriters' Lab and rewrote the script with David Olguín, a brilliant playwright and theatre director. Various friends of mine read it, including Alfonso Cuarón, Guillermo Arriaga, El Negro and Carlos Cuarón. All of them brought good ideas, but it was Carlos Cuarón who saw with great clarity how to resolve the problems, and gave the script the clear, solid structure that allowed me to concentrate on the actors and the filming. Basically my script moved between three levels: one was the captain of a Spanish galleon in the seventeenth century, caught in a storm in the Gulf of Mexico, his

The Mexican poster for *El Misterio del Trinidad* by respected director José Luis García Agraz

reflections and his prayers, his secret search for a son of his, lost in America. Another was the story of Juan Aguirre who faces up to his own life which is in turmoil, as well as his memories of his mother and father during his childhood in Veracruz. Carlos suggested telling the story in a linear fashion, without movements in time, in order to concentrate on the story of Juan, who, in the final version, became the core of the film. I wanted to create a story about fatherhood and forgiveness as a way of growing, maturing. The best adventures are, I think, the adventures of the heart.

Ana is a little girl who, very probably, has been raised in the absence as much of her mother as that of her father – a little girl who has gradually grown up by herself. Ana is both a reflection of what Isabel probably was, as well as the inheritor of the adventurer tradition of her dead grandfather, and, thanks to Juan's reconciliation with the memory of his father, Ana is the possibility of a better human being in the future.

Isabel is the mirror of Ana: beautiful but frustrated, intelligent but submissive to men – first her father, then her husband. She has ruled out the possibility of love and of motherhood. She has reached the edge by the time she meets Juan – who is her half-brother but also a reflection of her absent father. This double image of this man – and of her father – along with the possibility of seeing her childhood in Ana, provokes her 'inner torment', which will be sublimated through her incest, and the separation from a husband she doesn't love. She learns to grow late, but decides to grow in order to become herself. Her last steps in the film are the first towards her maturity.

I love genre films – distributors more so, because that way they avoid complex definitions. And I realize that in this case the mix of genres allowed me a greater range. The film starts out as a historical adventure, then becomes a melodrama with elements of comedy, and continues in this vein until it reaches the limits of tragedy, then becomes a contemporary adventure story, passes into Latin American magic realism and ends as all of one piece.

In Mexico it's very difficult to raise the initial funding to make a film, even more so if it's a personal project; so IMCINE's support was a basic requirement from the outset. However, in the course of five years, from the time I submitted my first treatment, IMCINE had five different Directors, and obviously that delayed the project. The film received approval under Alejandro Pelayo, predecessor to Alfredo Joskowicz, the present Director, but with much less funding – because money had run out under the previous administrations. So I began to look for other partners, and brought into the project anyone who could provide me with funds or contribute in kind. My creative independence was never compromised. In the end the co-production had many partners; and on the one hand IMCINE supported me with risk capital and, on the other, it lent me money at a preferential rate of interest – but that didn't make it any easier to pay the interest back.

One of the aspects of film-making I've loved ever since I was very young are the special effects created while filming, and miniatures. Good special effects are based on a key combination of trickery and calculated optical ratios. Obviously in Mexico such effects cost a fraction of what they cost in Hollywood, although it's also true that Hollywood can make an entire film out of special effects whereas we have to be very specific as to where they should be employed and to what extent they should be visible. There are limits beyond which effects can start to look cheap. My aim, therefore, right from the script stage, was to be very precise about the storms – i.e. to decide exactly what features they should have, and how they should be filmed to look as good as possible. I drew a very detailed storyboard for the storms as well as for the underwater shots.

The cabin of the galleon and almost all the interiors of the *Meridiano* were built at the Churubusco studios. The exteriors of the storm were filmed with the actors on the ship at anchor; some of the long shots were filmed at sea with a replica, others months later in a studio. It wasn't expensive, but it was laborious . . .

The film was nominated by the Spanish Academy of Art and Cinematographic Sciences for a Goya Prize in the category of Best Foreign Film in Spanish. I won the prize for Best Director at the Thirty-second Festival of Naval and Sea Films in Cartagena, in Murcia [Spain]. And the film received ten nominations from the Mexican Academy of Cinematographic Arts and Sciences, including Best Film, Best Director and Best Script. However, the distributors took a different view. They never believed in the film, despite investing $300,000. The launch displayed an almost complete lack of promotional planning, and the film came out in October 2003 and met with little success. IMCINE, the majority partner, pressed for the film to be kept showing in some cinemas outside Mexico City, and the National Film Theatre has put it on twice. But that's not enough in a medium dominated by American productions which are the top priority for the distributors that work in Mexico – Fox, Warner, UIP, etc.

7

21 Grams and *Hellboy*

Alejandro González Iñárritu, Alfonso Cuarón and Guillermo del Toro, Mexico's three most prominent contemporary directors, each made American films in 2003.

ROSA BOSCH *producer*: What's happened in Mexico is a great success story, and the achievements of Mexican film-makers have been phenomenal. Alfonso Cuarón directed *Harry Potter and the Prisoner of Azkaban*;[1] Alejandro [González Iñárritu] directed *21 Grams*; Guillermo [del Toro]'s *Hellboy* made it to number one at the US box office; Carlos Cuarón is busy both writing and directing – in fact, everyone is working. Because of this success expectations are very high. There is pressure on the film-makers, there is pressure on everyone.

JOSÉ LUIS GARCÍA AGRAZ *director*: Alejandro is a friend of mine. He's made two films to date, and has won over much of the world, be it audiences, or critics and film scholars, who can't help but notice the arrival of a 'whirlwind' on the filmic horizon. *El Negro* – as his friends call him – stamps his personality on his films in a way that few do; he's visceral, emotional, and has an instinct for form that makes people take to his films immediately. I think he has enormous talent and that a lot will be said about him in the course of his career; *Amores Perros* is just a taster; *21 Grams* is an exercise of the elements that mark the beginnings of the work of a director who is

[1] Released in 2004, *Harry Potter and the Prisoner of Azkaban* was the third in the increasingly popular film adaptations of J. K. Rowling's books. In this instalment, it's Harry's (Daniel Radcliffe) third year at Hogwarts, but a shadow looms. A reputedly dangerous mass murderer, Sirius Black (Gary Oldman), has escaped the Azkaban fortress and apparently has his sights set on revenge. Cuarón lent the project his customary visual panache and also imbued the film with a darker, more malevolent tone. This darker tone obviously didn't affect the box-office performance of the film, which to date has amassed in excess of $500 million at the international box office. On its opening weekend in Mexico, the film grossed over $1 million on 463 screens.

undoubtedly one of the most extraordinary directors to have appeared in contemporary cinema.

ALEJANDRO GONZÁLEZ IÑÁRRITU *director*: First of all I am not a diplomat nor an ambassador, and I am not paid by the government to represent my country. I am a very proud Mexican and I feel even more Mexican the further I go from my country. I feel more Mexican than a lot of corrupt politicians or bureaucrats. It is a great thing for an artist to travel, because it gives an even greater perspective of oneself and of one's country. In order to know yourself you have to explore other cultures. The people who do not feel this are suffering from a very reductive patriotism. Why is it that painters and writers can go and live and work in other countries but film-makers cannot? I think that a country is not a piece of land or a flag. A country is an idea that can be expressed through images, words and many other forms of expression. I feel very proud to be part of the community of world cinema and to tell whatever story I want to tell in whatever country.

I left my country, my house, my company and all the things that I had achieved up until that moment, including my commodities and the success with *Amores Perros*, to accept a self-imposed challenge. The move and the development and all of the possible things that can go wrong to make a film happen were very stressful. We arrived four days before 11 September and

Alejandro González Iñárritu and Rodrigo Prieto in Memphis: *21 Grams*

the vibe with Bush changed radically, not only in the US but also throughout the world. My kids felt alienated, and it took my wife and me a lot of time to get used to the city and to know who was who. It was like starting all over again, and consequently it was tough and stressful, as is anything that is really worth doing. Once I was fully immersed in it I didn't worry so much.

LEONARDO GARCÍA TSAO *critic/academic*: I think it's inevitable, in the sense that they get offered a lot of money and a lot of facilities to make their films there. When you have worked in Mexico, this must seem very attractive. I'm sure that later on you have regrets . . .

Del Toro makes fantastic horror movies, but this is a genre that's quite difficult to finance in Mexico. I'm sure he would love to do more Mexican projects where he would have more freedom, but the industry doesn't have the means or the financial structure to support him. Cuarón returned for *Y tu mamá también* and then made *Harry Potter and the Prisoner of Azkaban*. I do think Iñárritu is a very talented director. *21 Grams* was made with a lot of freedom, from a script that he had worked on with Guillermo Arriaga, so credit to him for keeping it on his own terrain.

ALEJANDRO GONZÁLEZ IÑÁRRITU: Guillermo [Arriaga] and I had such a good experience and such good results working together on *Amores Perros* that it was a natural decision for both of us to work again on the next script. However, the script of *21 Grams* was very difficult, much more ambitious, and this time the process of development with Guillermo was more complex. We were more conscious of the things that can go wrong, how easy it is to fail, and how difficult to get things right. This script was three years of going back and forth, and I involved as many people as I could to ensure that we approached it from all possible angles.

The title of 21 Grams *alludes to a mysterious loss of weight in the human body at time of death. Christina (Naomi Watts) is a recovered drug addict, happily married to an architect, with two lovely children. Paul (Sean Penn) is a mathematician dying slowly of a heart ailment, his relationship with Mary (Charlotte Gainsbourg) childless and increasingly loveless. Jack (Benicio del Toro) is an ex-convict who has embraced Christianity. These three individuals are brought together by a terrible accident, around which the screenplay moves freely in time. Much admired by audiences and critics alike, the film saw Oscar nominations for Del Toro and Naomi Watts.*

ALEJANDRO GONZÁLEZ IÑÁRRITU: At one point I reached a crisis and thought that I wouldn't make the film. I wasn't happy with the interior life of the characters and the way the structure and many other things were coming out of it. *21 Grams* was a radioactive material in which any false note, any little thing less or more than needed, could be fatal. The tone and the performances that I needed in order to make this film feel real and not over the top, because of the very nature of it, were very tough things to achieve, so the process with the script was very stressful and very delicate from my side.

GUILLERMO ARRIAGA *writer: 21 Grams* was originally written in Spanish and set in Mexico but it wasn't difficult for me to relocate it. I think the film deals with very primary and universal themes: love, hate, revenge, death and life. What the characters go through can happen to anyone in the world.

By then, I had travelled a lot through the US. I even travelled to Canada by bus, crossing the whole country border to border. And the work of a writer is to experience, to imagine, observe. I also had the great contribution of my translator, Alan Page, who helped me understand the best way to approach dialogue and American culture. Also I had the assistance of Patricia, my sister, who lived in New York for years and told me how Americans behave in certain circumstances.

As an atheist I can tell you that I am deeply concerned with human issues. As I think this is the only life we have for certain, I am convinced everyone has to value what surrounds you, specially your loved ones, and that we have to fight for life, value life, love life. So, as an atheist, my main goal is to live with a profound sense of love and sharing – since I will not get another chance.

ALEJANDRO GONZÁLEZ IÑÁRRITU: The main reason I relocated was that I wanted another challenge, and this gave me the opportunity to go to new territories. It really excited me and got me focused. I always focus more clearly when my adrenalin is running high. I think that you can know your idiosyncrasies much better, and your *Mexicanidad* from the outside, rather than just by living in the inside in your own little ranch of fear and prejudice. On a more personal note, the level of insecurity is very high in Mexico and to live in Mexico with two children was becoming very hard for me. Some people incorrectly thought that *Amores Perros* had made me a millionaire, and it was a little bit frightening dealing with the possibility of being kidnapped. Also, it's hard enough to make films in Mexico. It is equally hard to survive on the salaries directors are paid. The normal fee is about $40,000. When, as I do, you invest three years of your life in a project, this is not so much money. The main reason, however, is that, for this particular film, I wanted and needed to work with the very best actors in the world, and English was the universal language that would allow me this opportunity. I am not only talking about Americans, but French, Australians and Puerto-Ricans.

I decided that I did not want to shoot either in Los Angeles or New York because these cities have become like a set for me, I've seen them so many times on film that they're predictable. I needed a city that is not a 'movie city'. I also needed a city that I liked, that has a certain smell, a distinct personality and a unique quality. Thirdly, I needed a city far from Los Angeles and New York to get all these actors out of their houses and away from their wives and kids and friends. I wanted them to have no distractions from their work. I found all these things in Memphis. It also has a real history – a sadness that I guess is intrinsically linked with it being the birthplace of the blues.

I didn't show my project until it was completely finished, and when I say 'finished' I'm not talking about the script but *all* the other main decisions. That was because, as in *Amores Perros*, I didn't want anybody involved in the creative process more than Guillermo and myself. I financed the location scouting in several US territories, I started the casting process eight months in advance with Francine Maisler, and I got the three main actors attached to the project before any studio read a line from the script. That meant a lot to me as it meant that the actors were supporting me because they loved the script. They trusted me as a director and I considered them partners of the project. Ted Hope budgeted the film so when I presented the project to the five main studios I said to them, 'This is the script, these are the actors, these are the cities and this is the budget. I want complete creative control and final cut.'

Four of them were really interested in it and I just received support, respect and enthusiasm from all of them. In the end I went with Focus Features because some very good film-makers told me good things about David Linde and James Schamus. I was in total control of the creative process so I was as independent as on *Amores Perros* where I had a great experience with AltaVista films with Alejandro Soberón and Martha Sosa producing their first feature. I regard myself as an independent film-maker and when I work with a company I like to work with, not for, them because in that way the only beneficiary is the film itself.

GUILLERMO ARRIAGA: The idea of Paul's voice-over at the beginning and the end of the film came from an old unfinished novel I wrote when I was twenty-four and began with: 'So this is death, these ridiculous tubes, these needles . . .' And that's the way Paul's monologue begins. I considered this could help tell the story better. The screenplay needed a more committed point of view, and this monologue helps convey what the film is about.

ALEJANDRO GONZÁLEZ IÑÁRRITU: I felt that it was necessary to have a point of view. I pay a great amount of attention when I am blocking a film, and at various moments I found myself asking, 'Whose point of view is this? Is it Paul's; is it Christina's?' I felt that it was important at the end of the film to present very clearly one point of view. At the end the film it is like a memory for Paul and how he remembers events. I needed one leader, the one who redeemed the other two.

GUILLERMO ARRIAGA: Mary's and Paul's relationship was over a long time ago. The sad thing was that they were together because both of them were sick. He has the heart disease that limited his life, and she had this loneliness that was consuming her. He needs care and she needs someone to be with her. They both accept this situation, but when Paul has overcome his bad health through a new heart, things go back to where they were in the beginning. There is no love between them, just a convenient relationship. Without Paul's disease, they can no longer be together, and both they know it.

21 Grams: Sean Penn as Paul

Flaubert said, 'Madame Bovary, c'est moi . . .' All the characters have something to do with me. Jack is the English name for Santiago, my son's name; Marianne, his wife's character, is named after Mariana, my daughter, and Mary, Paul's wife, after my wife, María. Jack is maybe the one that fascinates me the most. As an atheist I am always surprised by religious fanaticism. How can someone be so much into God to the point that you lose absolute control of your life? I had a very close friend, an atheist also, who got married to a religious fanatic. She believed that anyone out of her sect was touched by the devil, so both of them decided not to relate to someone out of their religion. Suddenly my friend became a born-again Christian, obsessed with Jesus and God and the Devil. Jack also seduces me because he is the one who has been living with more pain. He is a character full of pain, not only after the accident, but also through all of his life. But I also have very strong links with Paul and Cristina. The three of them are obsessive, as I am.

My favourite moment in the screenplay is where Claudia shouts Christina's name, a moment we later learn to be the moment of the death of Christina's family. It represents all the strength of the tragedy, the moment when everything changes – it has this 'terribleness'. I couldn't avoid crying every time I wrote this scene. It really hurt me because it shows that tragedy is around us all the time, that it hides in the most unexpected places and it grabs you by the throat without any piety.

Christina is told 'Life goes on', and she refutes it, but this is the motif of the film and I wrote it on purpose; *21 Grams* is about the power of life over the power of death. Life has an enormous strength and it goes on even in the worst circumstances. When my son Santiago was five he asked me, 'If I die, will you ever smile again? Can you play again?' I was speechless. But he asked this question because his two-year-old cousin drowned in a swimming pool. And two or three years later his mom, my sister-in-law, was again smiling. Santiago couldn't understand – how could she smile after such an unbearable pain? So I wrote this film trying to answer his question for him.

ALEJANDRO GONZÁLEZ IÑÁRRITU: I think that one of the problems with cinema, and also with screenwriters – and this is where Guillermo really excels – is that they ask you to judge the characters. I never judge the characters; I always feel tenderness for them, always. No matter what they do, no matter who they are, I personally feel emotionally attached. This is one of the things that I really work on in the script. In *Amores Perros* El Chivo is a killer, but one of my goals was to make people understand this guy as a human being. This is imperative for me. This is also true of *21 Grams*.

21 Grams: Naomi Watts (Christina) and Alejandro González Iñárritu

You are emotionally drawn to the characters and want to follow them no matter who or what they are.

GUILLERMO ARRIAGA: Contradiction is for me the essence of human nature. The more contradictory someone is, the more human they appear to me. For example, Paul can look selfish in his relationship with Mary and absolutely generous with Christina. Jack is speaking of love all the time, and he mistreats his son. So I intended to avoid black-and-white characters in *21 Grams*. I don't believe in villains and heroes. I believe in the villain and in the hero that everyone has inside. I wanted the audience to feel compassion with Jack, the 'bad guy' that kills a family and runs away. I wanted them to understand an unfaithful character, as Paul, and to find out that a former drug addict can be a good mother.

ALEJANDRO GONZÁLEZ IÑÁRRITU: I wanted to make a film that's even more intimate and raw. I wanted it to be as direct as possible, and not at all stylized. Rodrigo and I wanted to disappear so people felt that there was no source lighting. I wanted the people to feel like they were looking at some images from a documentary, things that were captured in real time in a real way. I think that with this film Rodrigo touches your heart with every frame. He also really helped me to narrate the tale by pointing out details that proved to be extremely important. This is deliberately a very quiet and subtle film compared to the neurosis of *Amores Perros*. Fortunately there's more than one minute that I like in this film, especially in the performances . . . One of them is the moment where Sean Penn is asking the doctor if he is going to die after his new heart fails, because Sean's performance is remarkable. He expresses such fragility. Paradoxically I was really afraid of shooting the doctor scenes – and there are quite a few of them – because they are always so hard to get right and are frankly mostly unbelievable. Another moment is when Naomi Watts throws Sean out of her house after discovering the truth. Every time that I watched this scene I was moved by it. Naomi's range and honesty is unbelievable. I also like Benicio's simplest moments, such as his arriving home from gaol and kissing his little boy or at the end of the film when he's in the rural clinic asking Naomi for forgiveness just by looking at her.

I wasn't worried about the chronological order of the facts, but rather the emotional order of the events. I like that this film obligates you to judge again the same fact that you already saw before, and revise your prejudice. The editing phase was a very experimental and psychological time.

The people I work with are my family and my partners. It's an organic work and I hope that I can work for ever with these people. That way, you develop continuity and are able to grow together. I have been working with Rodrigo [Prieto] and Brigitte [Broch] for the last ten years and with Martín Hernández for twenty years. Memphis was like a Mexican invasion. Fortunately, after *Amores Perros* all of us continued to grow and learn more about our craft by working with others. Brigitte worked on various projects and Rodrigo worked with Spike Lee and Curtis Hanson on *The 25th Hour* (2002) and *8 Mile* (2002). Martín did the sound design for *City of God* (2002) and Gustavo Santaolalla and Aníbal Kerpel have just completed the music for Walter Salles's *The Motorcycle Diaries* (2004). When we all got together again, they were able to bring me the things they had learned and we returned to our roots.

RODRIGO PRIETO *cinematographer*: From the start we talked about the colours and what differences we could achieve. One thing we were struggling with is that we found that in America the colours weren't as vivid in terms of the interiors of houses as the colours they are painted outside. We had to adapt. In *Amores Perros* you see houses where the interior walls are very vivid blues and greens and this is the way that houses are in Mexico. We were struggling to keep strong colours in *21 Grams*, especially with the bleach-bypass process that produces colour. I used a little more colour in the

God's lonely man: Benicio del Toro as Jack Jordan in *21 Grams*

lighting this time. Paul's world is a little bluer to express his loneliness and his melancholy. His wardrobe was also designed to accentuate this and in the night lighting I use mercury vapour lights that are blue-green in hue. In Jack's world, where we went for more yellow and red tones, for the night lighting I used sodium-vapour type of lamps that give a very characteristic street lighting. Christina's world was more golden with a little red. When she goes back to her previous life of drugs we really pumped up the colour, with the lighting emphasizing amber, red and green.

Again, all of it was hand-held. Sometimes we used sandbags on top of a dolly. As with *Amores Perros* we wanted to have that breathing feel. The hand-held takes away the mechanical part of the camerawork to make it feel a little more organic. Also, in terms of the actual way that you work on the set, this way is much less obtrusive. You don't have obstructions such as a big dolly or tracks. You just light it, walk in with a camera and are ready to go. It's very helpful for the actors as well. As a cameraman, working hand-held is much more intuitive, there are no intermediates that you need to signal when you wish to move in for an extreme close-up.

BRIGITTE BROCH *production designer*: There was also a lot of Memphis reality. There is a lot of suffering still lingering in that city. The blues was born there and there are still clear racial and economic problems. We also wanted to capture the abandoned buildings and the exuberant vegetation that reminds you of sweat and passion. We looked at books by William Eggelston, juke joints, broken landscapes, and photographs by local artists.

RODRIGO PRIETO: I felt that we were initially trying too hard to make it not look like Memphis. When we were looking for locations within Memphis Alejandro would often feel loath to use somewhere that was too characteristic. We were feeling uncomfortable with that and I finally told Alejandro that we should embrace it. More and more we started accepting locations that had a very specific Memphis feel and texture without also trying to be too obvious about it. There were also some places that looked amazing that we didn't use because we thought that it was a bit much. It was a question of striking a balance.

The prison scenes were also very difficult because the space was so tight and enclosed. The actors and myself could barely all fit in the cell. Alejandro certainly likes to make me work hard. There were several other locations like this. When we shot in the bathroom in Paul's apartment I had to sit in the bathtub and then leap out at the moment Paul looks into the mirror. To get light in this sequence so that I was not then reflected in the mirror was very challenging but I really like this kind of challenge. When you are uncomfortable it probably means that it is a better shot.

On *21 Grams* Alejandro pretty much continued what he'd done on *Amores Perros* in terms of casting the actors and rehearsing with them. He doesn't choose actors dependent on their ability to help bring finance to the movie, or for their likely contribution to the box office. And I think the main reason Alejandro did *21 Grams* in the States was because of the actors: to tell that story, he wasn't sure that he would get what he had in his mind from only Mexican or Spanish actors. He approached it in a very similar way, taking his time and being very specific in terms of what he wanted from the performances and from each piece of dialogue.

It is amazing to watch Alejandro work; it is of an intensity that is almost spiritual. There is a deep respect for the actors, the emotions and for telling the story among the whole crew so I've learned to also get into this mode. With a camera you are so close to the actors and having to respond to them that you almost become an actor as well. It is very exciting. There becomes a point where you become a spectator and your job is a real privilege. Operating the camera you really are the first one to witness the performance and from the best angle. The camera is the best seat in the house. This feeling of privilege has happened to me on many occasions where you get a great ticket to see these incredible performances.

GUILLERMO ARRIAGA: I always describe this film as one about hope and love. How can someone overcome the deepest abyss? How can hope be found in the darkest places? I see this movie as the journey of three characters from hell to heaven and back to hell and then their struggle to come back. Jack comes from the hell of gaol and abuse, Christina from the hell of drug addiction and Paul from the hell of bad health. When they think that heaven has arrived, Jack through Jesus, Christina through her family and Paul with his new heart, circumstances throw them again to an even deeper hell. This is the theme of *21 Grams*: how can these characters find hope inside darkness; how can someone fight for life in a moment when death is striking with all its strength?

ALEJANDRO GONZÁLEZ IÑÁRRITU: I was interested in hope and I sincerely wish that I were able to convey this, as it is, I admit, a very intense and heavy film. I did struggle a lot in the editing and could see the film getting heavier and heavier. It was as if I were the pilot of a jumbo jet that was in danger of never taking off. I really tried to make the point that despite the intensity the characters were brave enough to confront their amazing losses.

My wife and I lost a baby two days after he was born. I dedicated *Amores*

Perros to Luciano, the son that we lost. *21 Grams* I dedicate to my wife. The presence of the absence is heavy.

I can tell you that there is no bigger loss than the one that Naomi's character suffers in the film. Some people have said that this is too much, but I say to them that life is like that. A friend of mine just recently lost his father and his sister to cancer. They died just two days apart. To put this in a film would feel as if you were making some terrible soap opera, but life is sometimes like that. There was a critic in Mexico who didn't like *21 Grams* and I told him that the reason he didn't like it was because he had nothing to lose. He has no wife, no children, not even a photograph of a dog or a plant. I feel that anybody who has something to lose or has already lost something can connect with this film.

I think that in the end I have an obsession and probably I will be repeating myself in different ways and times, but I definitely have a shadow that I project and I can't escape from it. The main difference between *Amores Perros* and *21 Grams* was that *Amores Perros* was three stories that intersected in an accident and *21 Grams* is only one story told from three different points of view. All these people reach a point where they stop living and merely begin to survive. How can you return to your life after such a moment? I think that redemption is not the end or an infinite state once you reach it, as many people believe. I think that it is just a temporary state, from which to begin again the strange cycle of life.

I would love to shoot in Mexico again. What has always helped me in my life is that I don't always know what I'm going to do, but I have always known what I am definitely not going to do. I can't imagine myself working to orders or the authority of another voice. In fact, I have a problem with authority, full stop. When somebody tries to interfere even a little bit in my process, it's very hard for me, so to submit to this machinery is not in my character. But you should never say 'never', because there could be some great novel's rights in the hands of the studio . . .

* * *

Guillermo del Toro enjoyed a big US hit in 2004 with Hellboy *(the film grossed over $60 million in the US alone). Based on the graphic comic by Mike Mignola, it concerns a demon raised from infancy by kindly surrogate father (John Hurt) after being conjured by and rescued from the Nazis; he grows up to become a defender against the forces of darkness. Photographed by Guillermo Navarro and starring Ron Perlman as the eponymous hero, the film is distributed worldwide by Columbia TriStar/Sony Pictures. Del Toro has just announced plans to direct a sequel in 2006.*

BERTHA NAVARRO *producer: The Devil's Backbone* really liberated Guillermo in terms of his being able to discern between personal projects on the one hand and studio assignments on the other. Interestingly, *Hellboy* is a real synthesis of both. It's a really personal project, but one made within the Hollywood structure. It's amazing that they let him do this very personal film with a huge budget but no stars. Guillermo is very happy with it.

GUILLERMO DEL TORO *director*: I work where I am allowed to – be that Spain, Prague, or the US. Wherever I go, however, I am a Mexican film-maker, and that is a fact that gets lost on the people who make these criticisms. They believe – in what is a form of ultimate racism – that if you leave then you are no longer 'one of us' and you're not going to come back. Well, Alfonso and I came back. Alfonso stayed and did *Y tu mamá* while I was rejected and went to do *The Devil's Backbone.* I was then rejected again, because even though *The Devil's Backbone* was half Mexican in terms of finance the authorities decreed that it was a Spanish film.

BERTHA NAVARRO: *The Devil's Backbone* opened things up in Hollywood for Guillermo. He was very at ease with himself after making this film, as it was very personal to him and that gave him the confidence to tackle a big-budget franchise with *Blade II* without striving to make it into a personal film.

Previously, del Toro's Spanish-language works had represented his more personal approach to film-making while the bigger-budgeted American studio projects – for one reason and another – saw the director mostly struggling to stamp his own personal vision on genre pictures. Hellboy, *however, muddied these waters.*

GUILLERMO DEL TORO: The only movie that truly blurs this line is *Hellboy.* This is really a combination of both.

Blade II was a very joyful experience. It was the opposite to *Mimic* in that I didn't have any aspirations to making a personal film and just wanted to give a personal touch to a movie that was unequivocally commercial. I was in total agreement with the producers and the studio on the movie we were making. On *Mimic* we were making two different movies. On *Blade II* I was very aware of what I was making and thoroughly enjoyed every minute of it. I was very afraid of fucking around with the screenplay too much because I understood that the franchise had its own rules.

The main thing was that I felt that I could exercise some muscles that I was going to need on *Hellboy.* Also, I have all my life made mid-term plans. When I was a kid I decided to study make-up so that I could set up my own

© Columbia Pictures

Giving evil hell: Ron Perlman (and 'friend') as the eponymous *Hellboy*

make-up company to allow me to do the effects for my own movie. After *Mimic* I said, 'I'm going to do my Spanish movie first and then I will do an American commercial movie and the two together will get my *Hellboy*.' Just like *The Devil's Backbone* was sixteen years in the wanting. I can tell you right now that my two favourite of my own films so far are *The Devil's Backbone* and *Hellboy*. I love them both and I could die a happy man just knowing that somewhere there are others who also like these two movies too.

The way I see the movies that I have done is that to me they are all one big movie that says, 'Hi, I'm Guillermo del Toro and I'm kind of ugly and disenfranchised.' *Hellboy* is ultimately what I think an atomic adventure-book movie could be and is very different from the other comic-book franchise and has a huge heart and a lot of beauty in the horror. It also has a lot of beautiful horror and very beautiful creatures and it's a celebration of otherness and being different. It is a Beauty and the Beast story where at the end they kiss and they both turn to beasts.

Some directors are very good at shooting dialogue, like Woody Allen or Quentin Tarantino, and I admire them, but when I do it it's so painful for me. My ideal movie would have no dialogue; it would just be a camera implicating the viewer in the action. I try to use the camera as if it were a curious child, always tiptoeing and trying to get a better view, but it keeps being pulled away, like when your mother is pulling you away from the scene of an accident but you keep rubbernecking to try to catch the last glimpse of the victim. I love to use the camera in this way to play with perspective. This occurs in *Cronos* where Ron Perlman is beating the crap out of Federico Luppi in front of the billboard. The camera pulls back a mile away, so that you see the whole billboard with them very tiny. I like to play hide-and-seek with the moment and be dragging the camera away just as the worst is about to happen. I have a killing in *Hellboy* that is very much like that. I have the camera in a position and then move it so that you go, 'Whoa, did I just see that or not?'

8
The State of Things

MARTHA SOSA *producer*: I believe that we cannot afford to lose this momentum within Mexico, and that my responsibility – and also the responsibility of our famous actors and directors – is to ensure that the international media know that we regard culture not as a luxury but as a *necessity*. That way, maybe, our government will also get this message. If we are known in the world, it's because of our culture: our books, our films, our music, our food. This is the only way we can last as a culture. It's the responsibility of the successful – the lucky – ones, and at the moment this is quite an extensive list that includes Alfonso Cuarón, Diego Luna, Arturo Ripstein, Guillermo del Toro, Gael García Bernal and Alejandro González Iñárritu. These are the ones who have to really open their mouths – because, as you know, nobody listens to producers. And thankfully, they are doing it.

ALFONSO CUARÓN *director*: I hate it when people talk of all that is happening as part of the changes post Vicente Fox. It was all already going on, actually. Fox is merely a by-product of the changes that are going on in this country. He was chosen and elected not because of Vicente Fox, but because people were pissed off with the PRI, and Fox himself knows this. On the other hand, I don't have the perception that Fox is a crook, as opposed to our previous president. I don't think he's corrupt. Maybe he is and I'm being naive. But then I don't agree necessarily with the way he is trying to handle our country as if it is a corporation.

ÁNGELES CASTRO *Director,* CCC: I think we had expectations, perhaps *naive* expectations, regarding the Fox government. One of our main expectations was that in a cultural sense we would have the same level of support. At this time, culture is not a priority. Because the country is suffering terrible economic problems.

GUILLERMO DEL TORO *director*: To be honest, our current president is not unlike our other presidents in his lack of interest in culture.

We almost had a very sad epilogue about the Mexican industry when they were trying to exterminate IMCINE and the CCC. And I said to people that we had to all be united, or together as an industry we would all go to hell. Those events were a warning sign. I repeat again: we should be united to form a strong front and we should not underestimate the value of having all film-makers standing firm together.

I do not say this in the poetic way of 'I would like to teach the world to sing' but it really should be a much needed call to arms.

Vicente Fox initially appeared supportive of the film industry – a support that included the announcement of an initiative to boost local film production by applying a one peso levy to all cinema admissions, with the intention of channelling monies raised directly into local production. However, the initiative provoked outrage from Motion Picture Association President Jack Valenti and was swiftly withdrawn.

ALFREDO JOSKOWICZ *film-maker/Director,* IMCINE: The Mexican Congress passed a 1 per cent box office levy on ticket sales at the Mexican box office. In 2002 Mexican exhibitors sold something in the region of a hundred and fifty million tickets at an average cost of $3 so we expected to have $15 million dollars for our two funds, FOPROCINE and FIDECINE. The reaction of Motion Picture Association President Jack Valenti was immediate. He sent a letter to President Vicente Fox saying that they felt violated because the Mexican Congress did not consult with them over the decision. In January of this year the five major studios took legal action and issued the Mexican government with a lawsuit. It is currently going through the courts, but I do not think that the money will be coming. We in the film community are all outraged, but we have to follow the legal process, which is lengthy. So we are trying to divert our energies to finding other possible avenues of finance. It is interesting that in Brazil large corporations make tax contributions to national film production.

Fox's institutional overhaul then became much clearer on 12 November 2003. In an announcement to Congress that provoked howls of outrage both within the industry and throughout the international film community, Fox proposed plans to end the Mexican government's decades-long involvement with the industry by dissolving both IMCINE *and the* CCC *and selling off the Churubusco Azteca studios. In an open letter to the government, artistic and intellectual commentators and film-makers including González Iñárritu, Alfonso and Carlos Cuarón and Salvador Carrasco vehemently opposed Fox's intentions. Fox's measures were subsequently abolished, with continued support pledged to all three institutions.*

JOSÉ LUIS GARCÍA AGRAZ *director*: Although attributed to Goebbels, it was actually Hanns Johst, the Nazi head of the German Writers' Union, who said, 'When I hear the word "culture", I reach for my revolver.' In Mexico, though, we don't need bullets to threaten or demolish culture. You need look no further than the law itself for the means of exterminating, for example, an institution whose specific function is the promotion and dissemination of culture, or a school dedicated to the education of future Mexican artists. The means to do this are dissolution, liquidation, extinction, merger or expropriation.

As well as the institutes and funds that support cinematographic activity, the Fox government proposed the 'de-incorporation, liquidation, extinction or merger' of Notimex, the official news agency, the Colegio de Posgraduados de Chapingo which makes strategic studies of the Mexican countryside, the earth, etc., and of the Prónosticos para la Asistencia Pública, a public-health-authority research institute.

The proposal suggested that 'faced with a shortage of budgetary funds for the coming year', 'a series of measures as regards de-incorporation, rationalization, and budgetary austerity' be carried out 'in order to generate savings that allow the increase of expenditure destined to programmes of social and economic benefit that carry priority'.

IMCINE is the sole public body that still provides financial support for cinematographic creation and creators – an activity that has clearly moved to the private sector. That is how cold, insensitive and lacking in historical perspective managerial thinking becomes when it is not accompanied by the slightest interest in art and culture. In an ideal world, public servants would be both good administrators and people sensitive to artistic creation.

ALEJANDRO GONZÁLEZ IÑÁRRITU *director*: When it was suggested to Churchill that he should close the museums and stop the funds for every cultural project because the country needed money for the war, his response was that if we sell this and close that, then what we are fighting for?

Mexico is a country of miracles. In fact, it's a miracle that we're even still alive because there are so many things that have to be solved. Everybody is talking about the hot things that are happening in Latin American cinema, and in Mexican cinema in particular, and I feel ashamed about this because I know that *nothing* is happening. This is the problem. All these films that have been made by people such as myself, Alfonso Cuarón, Carlos Bolado or Carlos Reygadas are quite simply miracles that have exploded.

In poor countries such as mine, art is a secondary need; people should come first, and I agree with that. But if the money that we pay in taxes goes towards food, education, medicine and all of the things that they say the money is going towards, everything will be all right. But the problem is that our politicians are the shame of the nation. They spend millions of dollars in costly presidential campaigns they fight between one party and the other without any result, solution, ideas or straight planning for the country. By so clearly favouring the television industry over the cinema industry, these self-same politicians forget that the cinema industry can create a lot of employment, exportation and very positive cultural and economic consequences. With just with 2 per cent of what they stole or 1 per cent of what they spend to promote themselves, we could have a powerful industry.

BERTHA NAVARRO *producer*: I do think that institutions such as IMCINE should be there to help film-makers, especially first-time film-makers. But the contradiction is that they are also producers, and I think that an Institute should nourish and help make films, but not itself be actively involved in making them – as they can only reflect the dominant ideology of the state. The increased freedom of speech in Mexico remains inextricably linked to the rise of the independent producer. Independent film-making is more open to freedom.

CARLOS CUARÓN *writer/director*: If you have a good solid project, then one of the private production companies is going to take it. The majority of the films that go through IMCINE become stuck in production: the pre-sales are not good, and on some the quality is not that good, and none of the private investors want to share the risk. As a film-maker, my point of view is that IMCINE should produce only short films or features by first time directors. IMCINE should certainly not produce beyond this, or even distribute.

What the state *could* do for cinema

GAEL GARCÍA BERNAL *actor*: According to the media, Mexico is one of the hottest spots right now talent-wise – but it is also one of the hardest places for film in terms of economics and indigenous industry. Other Latin American countries such as Brazil and Argentina are constantly introducing legislation to support their national cinema, and all despite their own fragile economies. This is very inspiring, and something I think that Mexico should learn from. Cinema in Mexico *can* be sustainable and it *can* be an industry and it *can* become a major source of revenue for the country.

ÁNGELES CASTRO: I think that if the state is not going to support cultural endeavours then it has to make law in order to stimulate private investment. Without this legislation, it is a huge risk for private investors to participate in cultural projects, because many of these projects have no way of recouping their investments, meaning that there's no reason to conduct business.

GUILLERMO ARRIAGA *writer*: It is all connected to the distribution of the peso at the box office. The exhibitors take a very large chunk; the distributors a chunk, leaving very little to return to the producer. To have a successful Mexican film for the producer, the box office must reach at least $7 million. That is a *lot* of money.

JOSÉ LUIS GARCÍA AGRAZ: For some years now, the various cinematographic sectors have wanted to undertake a full-scale restructuring of the industry. We want the institutions to function more efficiently. We want a new division of box-office receipts. The producer, the party that has taken the most risks, receives the least. That's why there are no producers who want to risk their money in such a disadvantageous manner. It means the only sectors that grow are the cinema owners – in their majority linked to American chains – and the distributors, Fox, Warner, UIP, Buena Vista, etc. And we all know what interests they respond to.

GUILLERMO DEL TORO: We are fighting trans-national companies, companies that are very aware that Mexico is an incredibly important market, and it is important that legislation changes at a federal level in order for our industry to survive. Mexico has an incredibly rich heritage and history of great movies in all genres, and to let our identity in cinema be lost would be a tragedy.

JOSÉ LUIS GARCÍA AGRAZ: What is required is a law like in France or Spain – and now in Brazil and Argentina – that gives incentives at the box office, that exempts films from tax, that displays an awareness of the importance of having a national film industry that is strong and competitive, which means having more freedom to create and incentivize national production. But everything indicates that the majority of this government's civil servants are ignorant of what art is, and that, among other things, it serves to satisfy needs that go beyond man's animal nature. And woman's. And children's.

As one of our great writers, Fernando del Paso, has recently pointed out:

We have a government that does not know what culture is. That does not understand it. That is unaware that the various manifestations of Mexican culture are – and have been for many years – the most valuable part of our exports. And the part that is the most precious and the most appreciated by people around the world.

We have a government that does not know – and if it does it prefers to hide the fact – that the Mexican institutions charged with promoting and disseminating our culture, within and beyond our borders, have paltry budgets, which, if eliminated, would make no real contribution to the savings the Executive intends to achieve, but would achieve this: paltry savings. But the cost, to the development of our cultural wealth, would be immense.

We have a government that does not understand – and if it does it prefers to say nothing – that these institutes and schools were not set up to generate profits. They are not businesses. They are not companies. They are not Coca-Cola. They are bodies for long-term investment, which is recouped, and richly so, when they carry out their functions properly. They invest in the talent of the Mexican people, and they are successful when this talent bears its fruit. On many occasions, as is well known, IMCINE recoups a good part of its financial investment. On some, everything. IMCINE's money is not given away lightly.

We have a government that intends to generate savings in order to increment expenditure destined for programmes of a social benefit, which have priority, but which ignores – or pretends to ignore – the fact that culture – like education – also represents a social good. Although I doubt that the majority of our government's functionaries have ever received the benefit of culture.

RODRIGO PRIETO *cinematographer*: Look at *Alexander* (2004). We have British, French and Dutch money, and it's because of the tax breaks that we are shooting in England and bringing money into the country. This is the kind of thing that should be happening in Mexico – not considering closing down IMCINE and the film schools. Why not instead give tax breaks and incentives to the producers, so that we can sustain what is a very important and obviously very creative industry? The industry, a major boost to culture, could potentially also give a major boost to the Mexican economy.

DANIEL BIRMAN *producer*: The main obstacles are the same as always; production costs are high and the sharing out of the income is much less favourable for the producer. Distributors and exhibitors really take the biggest share of the pie, but there is always a film or two that passes the 1 million attendance and makes a profit. My grandfather has always impressed on me the huge risk involved in producing, not only in Mexico but also worldwide. He says, 'If I knew what films would do huge business, I would leave the producing part, and just charge to give advice.'

ROSA BOSCH *producer: Japón* was actually very aggressively marketed internationally. But if we are talking of these more niche titles within Mexico, then no matter how in love with a film one may be, the reality of the matter is that rules and regulations don't ensure that these films get the exhibition support they perhaps deserve. There are legal protections that we as producers all want, and there is a very open-door policy that is the result of regulations being lobbied for by producers such as Bertha Navarro, to make sure that locally produced pictures do get a fair crack of the whip compared to more obviously commercial titles, American or otherwise. But look at the UK. Even with the various film bodies that exist here, particularly the Film Council, this doesn't necessarily provide a cinema that is entirely active and fully culturally diverse.

LEONARDO GARCÍA TSAO *critic/academic*: Like everybody else throughout the world, we in Mexico have been overtaken by Hollywood. The audience has been conditioned by Hollywood, so when we get films from Spain or Argentina the audience doesn't want to go and see them. Even Almodóvar isn't successful in Mexico. *All About My Mother* (1999) didn't do any business here. It comes down to the fact that Mexican audiences want to see only a handful of Mexican films and the rest of the time will watch films only made by Hollywood.

This is a problem of education and culture and if the official stance on culture is negligence then this is part of the problem. We also have several large television companies taking their cue from the rest of the world to produce mass-market reality TV shows that are in danger of rendering audiences brain dead.

ALFONSO CUARÓN: I believe in the responsibility of the government to support culture, and to fund and help IMCINE. The problem with Mexican cinema is the lack of continuity. When I raised this issue about the sustaining of a Mexican cinema industry six years ago, the bureaucrats at IMCINE told me that there was only one true film industry in the world and that is Hollywood; the rest are just film communities. I told them that I disagreed. You have France, you have Spain, you have England, you have India, and you have Hong Kong. What they wanted was to control the industry completely, not to regenerate it.

What is very encouraging in Mexico is when, as has happened, the biggest film of the year is not an American film, it is a Mexican film. That shows willingness.

ROSA BOSCH: Mexico is now one of the top three emerging countries in terms of cinema attendance, so the rate of growth of the whole audio-visual sector has been phenomenal and there has been an explosion in the number of cinema screens. Financial analysts can now see that, as a business, cinema in Mexico is becoming viable, which will inevitably trigger further private investment. This is, of course, in conjunction with a group of film-makers who have really been able to deliver the goods. By the same token, the film-makers have more energy and more imaginative scope to devote to their films because they are no longer subject to the pitiful funds available from IMCINE or any other bureaucratic organization.

ALFREDO JOSKOWICZ: So we are all fighting and discussing, especially right now as we have something like 70 per cent of our talent in Mexico without jobs. I am constantly, with the help of my minister, asking for production funds.

The demands of the Mexican audience

DANIEL BIRMAN: Right now there's a huge need from Mexican audiences to see Mexican cinema, and what they want to see is what they are living. I really don't think that it varies that much from class-to-class or region-to-region; the shared experience is often the same, and so these audiences are closely linked. There is a need for Mexican cinema to reflect our culture and our lives with all their various idiosyncrasies. That said – and I think this is universal and not just confined to Mexican films – people do not want to go to the cinema only to suffer. I think a very important aspect of film-making is to consider for whom you are making the films. I don't believe that a director should make a film only to satisfy their own views and desires. I believe you must be tolerant of the audience and differing perspectives, without sacrificing your own point of view.

HUGO RODRÍGUEZ *director*: I've always said to my students that if we don't devote at least a small part of our thinking to the person who will see our creation, we shouldn't complain afterwards when no one comes to the cinema to see our work. I believe in individual creativity and in experimenting, but you have to be a mature artist – and obviously I'm not speaking only in terms of age – to meet the challenges that these works represent.

In 2001 Daniel Birman founded Arthaus Films. Prior to Arthaus, art-house distributors were releasing only two or three 'specialized' titles per year.

DANIEL BIRMAN: We implemented a strategy to tackle the lack of diversity faced by Mexican cinema-goers. We founded Arthaus with this philosophy in mind, and it worked. People are eager to see all kinds of stories, not only action and special-effects films. I think the most important part of being a distributor is to show the audience what they want to see. Unfortunately there are many wonderful films out there every year that are almost impossible to market; therefore we are forced to 'sacrifice' many of them. But our idea of bringing good-quality films was made, basically, because it was predominantly art and foreign-language pictures that were being sacrificed.

We have proved that there is a market for our films. And exhibitors have also seen this. Therefore we've established special circuits of five to fifteen cinemas in Mexico City, and probably another fifteen to twenty throughout the rest of Mexico to show our movies. And it has turned out very well for all of us. I believe that all Mexican films should be able to have a theatrical life. That is one of the reasons I firmly opposed the plans to sell IMCINE. Even though I believe that it's not the best distribution channel in Mexico, it is still a distribution outlet for not-so-commercial films, and a valuable resource through which these films can be screened in the traditional manner in movie theatres.

The Latin American Spanish-language dimension

EMMANUEL LUBEZKI *cinematographer*: We have had such renaissances before, and they have always died. I think that we have right now a great talent pool of writers, directors, actors, cinematographers, production designers, etc., but what we also have, and what we have not had before, is a massive amount of people speaking Spanish who also happen to have money. It's also important that the biggest minority in the United States speaks Spanish and so now all of the studios are moving towards making low-budget movies that can make millions of dollars in these markets. For the first time in many years we potentially have a great business.

ROSA BOSCH: From a purely business point of view, I guess there's a strong case for saying that this has happened against the background of Latin America as a continent accelerating its growth in regard to cinema distribution, box office, and increased and improved screens. There is clearly development throughout all of Latin America, not just Mexico. Plus, the rest of the world is really paying attention. Latin American cinema has not had this kind of attention for many years.

FRANCISCO GONZÁLEZ COMPEÁN *producer*: AltaVista has been reconfigured but I am still involved with the company through some of the projects that I originally began to develop there. I have started Draco Films, my own production company. I'm not so sure how we're going to do it, but we do want to break into the US market and are trying to develop films that could be marketed in America. There is the Latin way and the crossover way and I think that both ways should be explored very conscientiously.

BERTHA NAVARRO: We used to focus only on 'Mexican films', but now I am co-producing with Chile and Ecuador and I hope in the near future to also have a project in Argentina. I think that the goal now, and certainly with a film that I have just produced in Ecuador,[1] is to make the best Spanish-speaking films. It's not only Mexican films. This tendency of working with other non-Mexican director and actors is something that I think will grow for Latin American producers: it's a new way of enabling us to tell our stories, and also a way of making the Spanish-speaking market even stronger.

To achieve this, we need to have a wider distribution and to make sure we have presence at all the international markets. It is so difficult to do any film that is not in the English language. I think that we could be potentially the most important market. As a language Spanish is spreading beyond the Spanish-speaking countries, and we have a huge Latin community in the States. Also, throughout Europe there is an increased awareness of Spanish-language products. This is in part due to the status of prominent Spanish cinema auteurs such as Pedro Almodóvar. What is happening now is something that feels evolutionary and very natural. This is also reflected in the renewed pride that people in Latin American countries have for their cinema. This is very much the case in Mexico where audiences are once again watching Mexican movies and taking satisfaction from them. I also think that the Mexican audience is like any other audience in that there is a growing sense of fatigue when faced with the same Hollywood films. It is not

[1] Directed by Sebastián Cordero, *Crónicas* screened to great acclaim at the 2004 Cannes Film Festival. The film concerns the star of a sensationalistic Miami news show who travels to the Ecuadorian coastal village of Babahoyo to cover the story of a serial killer who hunts children. When his personal ambitions gets out of hand, tragic consequences ensue.

just Mexican films that are being more widely shown in Mexico but distribution is also opening up for Spanish and other European films. This was not the case four years ago.

Produccións Anhelo is the production company Cuarón set up with business magnate Jorge Vergara.

ALFONSO CUARÓN: We created this company to do *Y tu mamá* and in the process of doing the film we talked about putting together a company in the States, which we now have called Monsoon. It was actually Jorge's initiative, saying, 'You are forgetting about Latin America', and 'Though you have it easy there are a lot of people who don't.' So we said, 'Let's go for it.' The idea is to not only do Mexican films but also films in Spanish. We will develop Mexican projects but we also want to be open, just like they did in Asia, so that it was not only about Hong Kong cinema but also about the areas around. We also have something that is priceless that even the Asians don't have: a shared language. If we can create a circuit of films from Mexico, Argentina, etc., then it is going to be healthier for everybody. That doesn't mean to lose the individual or national voices – I hate the word 'national' – but certainly the individual voices from each culture.

Mexicans in Hollywood/globalization

ÁNGELES CASTRO: I have been thinking a lot recently about globalization. It would be better, I think, to view it in a positive way rather than bemoaning it. It is good that Mexican directors and film artists can leave to work in America, but most do come back. Look at Alfonso Cuarón and Emmanuel Lubezki and *Y tu mamá también*. Cuarón is also developing another project to be shot here in Mexico. Look also at Alfonso Arau and Luis Mandoki, who are both going to be shooting pictures here.

CARLOS CUARÓN: OK, Alfonso [Cuarón] made *Harry Potter and the Prisoner of Azkaban*; Alejandro [González Iñárritu] made *21 Grams*; [Guillermo] del Toro made *Hellboy*; so Carlos Reygadas is the only one working in Mexico City. But after *Harry Potter*, Alfonso is coming back to Mexico because we have other projects.

EMMANUEL LUBEZKI: Because we have often worked in an environment where there is no supporting industry, it's easy to develop your own distinctive voice. In the States that's more difficult, because there is such a strong industry, and it has certain standards, and consequently there's a fear of experimentation. Working in the States, I have less chance to experiment. It's just more difficult for an author to find a voice in America than it is in Mexico. In the States you don't have any freedom but, on the other hand, you have everything else. In Mexico it is very different. You, the film-maker, are very poor, almost to the extent that you don't have the tools to do the job. What you *do* have is complete freedom, and this freedom is undoubtedly a big plus.

ROSA BOSCH: The current level of craftsmanship and talent in Mexican cinema is astonishing. One can perhaps be unfair to Arturo Ripstein's generation, because they simply didn't have this level of technical excellence; and they certainly didn't have casts of the calibre of Gael García Bernal, Diego Luna and Salma Hayek, actors who are able to get even the major studios excited.

Felipe Cazals has made only one film in eight years. Paul Leduc hasn't made a feature in something like ten years. The only one who has had a wider output is Arturo Ripstein. And, in a way, Ripstein was at a very interesting, if you like, blossoming moment in Mexican cinema with *Profundo carmesí*. Since then he seems to have worked mainly in video. These directors have simply been overtaken. Ripstein and Leduc would consider themselves *auteurs* in the sense that, for example, Theo Angelopoulos is an *auteur*. And this perhaps can be a dangerous thing. Though their films have screened at international festivals, they haven't had the same kind of sustained publicity enjoyed by films directed by Cuarón, del Toro and González Iñárritu. Those directors have their films released commercially on a massive global scale, and this obviously sustains their reputation and increases their exposure. In some ways it's sad to say this, but inevitably there has been a takeover – not a handover, a takeover.

BERTHA NAVARRO: The pressure you have as a film-maker now is how to make sure that your films are more commercial and can be appreciated by a wider audience.

But I must also add that it's my belief that you should be able to make any film you want. If there is a healthy industry, it should sustain the *auteurs* and those making more personal expressions. Not every film should be made because of its potential to generate box office. But the circumstances, the economics and the general market are so against us that you have always to have an eye on commercial success.

ALFONSO CUARÓN: It's so important that though Guillermo, Alejandro and myself can now work anywhere in Hollywood, we still are able to find our individual voices. There are other film-makers who have continuity and make a film year after year, such as Ripstein. I mean, you may not like the films but ultimately they have an audience, even though there is no pretence of their regenerating the industry. And yet ultimately Ripstein is a film-maker with an undeniable international presence. Ripstein is not reaching out to audiences and probably couldn't care less about audiences. It is about having an eloquence that is accessible. It is important to differentiate between the industry and cinema, but we must never forget that the healthier the industry the more possibilities for cinema.

JOSÉ LUIS GARCÍA AGRAZ: There are extraordinary Mexican film-makers who don't yet have a worldwide reputation. Ignacio Ortiz Cruz is a director from Oaxaca and a graduate of the CCC, writer and director of *La Orilla de la tierra* (*The Edge of the Earth*, 1994) and *Cuento de hadas para dormir a los cocodrilos* (*Bedtime Fairy Tale for Crocodiles*, 2002).

BERTHA NAVARRO: I think this is a really interesting period for women directors in Mexico. There is an amazing documentary film [*Recuerdos* (*Remembrance*, 2003)] made by Marcela Arteaga, a first-time film-maker and graduate of the CCC. There was also *Perfume de violetas* (2001) by Marisa Sistach. This was a lower-budget film but it was very hard hitting in its depiction of rape and it didn't have the luxury of a huge marketing campaign or a recognizable soundtrack and yet it still managed to find a very good audience.

LEONARDO GARCÍA TSAO: *Perfume de violetas* was quite successful. The film is very much in the league of hard-hitting films about the under-privileged classes and is, I think, Marisa Sistach's best work to-date.

GUILLERMO DEL TORO: In 2001 Alfonso Cuarón – with *Y tu mamá* – and I – with *The Devil's Backbone* – were both hoping our movies would be selected to represent Mexico in the Foreign Film category at the Oscars. I was confident that Alfonso was going to get the majority of the vote, and he felt that I was going to. We spoke the night before the decision was to be announced to wish each other luck, and I told him that if he got it, I would be as happy as if my film had been selected. Of course, the next morning we realized that neither of us had got it.

CARLOS CUARÓN: Marisa Sistach's *Perfume de violetas* was the film they selected, and actually Alfonso and I always said that *Perfume* was in many ways the better film. But, you don't send the best movie to the Academy –

Ximena Ayala and Nancy Gutiérrez in Marisa Sistach's *Perfume de violetas*

you send the one that they're going to like and that has a chance of winning.

ROSA BOSCH: It's the same everywhere – behind all of these great guys is a great woman. Remember also that women have not just been behind the scenes. Mexico has produced great women directors, such as Marisa Sistach, María Novaro, and Dana Rotberg. That said, I don't want to be led down the feminist route. Women producers and directors have not had it easy in Mexico, but there is sexism everywhere, and in Mexico 'the boys' have also had a tough time directing and getting their films made. What I will say is that all those years of feminism have given women the right to have a family and a career, whereas before they had to choose between the two. The truth of the matter is that in terms of the roles women perform, there have always been fewer women directors than producers, and I really don't know why. I think it's fair to say that within the film industry the majority of roles performed by women are in either PR, marketing, distribution, line producing, or as heads of production in arts and crafts departments. I think that women make very good producers because, in a way, what we are essentially doing is babysitting – both financially and artistically.

The year 2003 saw Gael García Bernal take lead roles in Walter Salles's film about the young Che Guevara, The Motorcycle Diaries, *and Pedro*

Almodóvar's Bad Education. *Bernal can make an economic success of a Mexican project. He also has acquired a spokesman-like status for Mexican cinema in general.*

GAEL GARCÍA BERNAL: It's a tough ride, but it really allows me to reinvent the rules of the game, and often for good. For example, being an actor from Mexico, I perhaps have a freedom that an actor in Hollywood might not have. I'm able to make surprising and uncompromising choices. I do feel an intense responsibility, but I also feel a responsibility towards enjoying my position – and to also being grateful for it. It's a drive, for me, to do the films I want to do, not only because of the consequences that may arise because of them but to also reaffirm why I originally wanted to act.

MARTHA SOSA: Gael is a bona-fide superstar; I would put him in the same league as Marcello Mastroianni now. He's been offered lots of American films. Now he is shooting his first American film, James Marsh's *The King*, an independent feature. I have no doubt that 2004 will be both Gael's and Diego's international year as the films they have made will be seen everywhere. With both Gael and Diego I think it is a case of having waited for the right project to come without fear and working very hard. It has been important to them that they very carefully hand-pick the people that they are going to work with and they are both monitoring their careers very carefully and also have the benefit of having very good American agents.

Diego made *Frida* (2002), his first American studio project; he then made *Open Range* (2003) with Kevin Costner. Then he completed *Dirty Dancing: Havana Nights* (2004). He has also been shooting *Criminal*, a Steven Soderbergh and George Clooney production that is a remake of *Nine Queens*.[2] He has taken a very big step in a very short time. It was between *Open Range* and *Dirty Dancing: Havana Nights* that he made *Nicotina*.

Last words: future prospects

LEONARDO GARCÍA TSAO: I am pessimistic by nature, but Mexican cinema has survived the very worse of times. Think back to the 1980s. The situation was even bleaker than now and yet the cinema managed to survive. I have always said that Mexican film-makers are like cockroaches – not in a

[2] Directed by Fabián Bielinsky, *Nine Queens* (*Nueve Reinas*) is a gripping, stylishly shot heist thriller that could be considered to Argentinian cinema what *Amores Perros* is to Mexican cinema.

derogatory sense I must add, but in that they can survive anything. They have a very strong survival instinct. I think that emerging technologies such as Digital and High-Definition will be a salvation for Mexican cinema. We have seen a lot of films recently made digitally. Even Ripstein has done it.

BERTHA NAVARRO: These guys – especially the directors such as [Guillermo] del Toro, Alfonso Cuarón and [Alejandro] González Iñárritu – have very clear ideas of what they want to do and they will go where they have to go to do it. It is important to point out, however, that all three of these directors – and these three are undoubtedly the biggest director figures right now in Mexican cinema – have started producing, and use their influence to discover and nurture other young directors. This is their way of being linked to the Mexican cinema.

ALFONSO CUARÓN: To summarize everything, this 'wave' is an effect of what is happening in the arts in Mexico and not just film. It is a generation reclaiming its part in the world, and not only in Mexico – and this doesn't make you less Mexican. There is a big fear of the old guard, and there are a lot of criticisms of people such as myself and Guillermo that we are selling out and that we're not good Mexicans. I think that you can be universal and still be a good Mexican.

What I find very exciting about Alejandro, Guillermo and Carlos Reygadas is that what we are talking about is a generation and what I am talking about here is not age but minds. There are Mexican film-makers, artists, scientists, entrepreneurs who want to reclaim their position in the world, not only in Mexico.

CARLOS CUARÓN: The Mexican media speaks of a renaissance every six years. It's due to the fact that we change government every six years. IMCINE changes hands and new people make movies, but that's about it. There is no true renaissance. What is happening within Mexico is that there are four or five very bright film-makers, and now most of these are abroad. I am speaking of course of my brother Alfonso, Alejandro González Iñárritu, Guillermo del Toro and Carlos Reygadas, who is doing his specialized art films – actually, I think *Japón* is the best Mexican film in a very long time. It's a similar thing in terms of cinematographers. You have Chivo [Emmanuel Lubezki], Rodrigo Prieto, and maybe three or four others, and they are all now abroad. We also have a big problem with writers because we have never had a huge writing tradition in Mexico in terms of film-making. The ones that we had during the 1940s and 1950s – the Golden Age – were mostly Spaniards that came with the Civil War. Strong writers that are writing and writing also outside of Mexico City are probably only Guillermo Arriaga – for me the best – and then myself. The rest are suffering, and perhaps teaching, because it's very difficult to survive as a writer here.

MARTÍN SALINAS *screenwriter*: I've been involved in teaching, and I still am, though not on a regular basis: I travel a lot, so what I usually do is to get involved in one- or two-week labs or workshops. Being in touch with the new generation of screenwriters and directors from all over Latin America is an extremely nurturing experience to me. In many cases I have continued re-reading the new drafts of scripts that have been brought to that lab, and making notes for the writers up to the final draft. Although I do think that a good story is a good story no matter what the language or culture, I also think that we do need to work hard to dig within our own cultural background and language to explore our roots. My mother, who studied literature, would make me laugh with joy by reading fragments to me of *El Lazarillo de Tormes* and *El Quijote* by the bedside when I was a child, or quote Lope de Vega or Francisco Quevedo, with their sharp angles and notes on human nature. You'll never get something like that from a screenwriting manual published in LA . . .

CARLOS CUARÓN: I'm always optimistic. I believe in talent, so, even though I think we are in something of a crisis regarding talent, I do think there are kids either in high school or film school and even drop-outs who will contribute to film culture. I know this because I am already starting to meet some of them. With Jorge Vergara,[3] Alfonso has a production company here in Mexico and I work in the company as a creative producer. My role is to work very closely with the head of development, nurturing the young talent he finds. Most of these people are very young, and I want to believe in these people I have been meeting in the last two years.

GUILLERMO DEL TORO: The tragedy of Mexico is that we do have the human resources; we don't have the structure to support them. Alfonso, Alejandro and I are part of a panel of judges in a contest that happens every year on the radio. We basically award cash to short films on an annual basis. In those shorts, I have seen a lot of people who I am absolutely sure will eventually become very good film-makers. If you don't water your roots, then you will go dry. It is incredibly important that Bertha, Alejandro and I continue

[3] The producer of *Y tu mamá también*, Jorge Vergara is a visionary Mexican businessman who in 1991 founded Omnilife de Mexico SA, a company that creates products for healthy living.

producing. I was talking to Alejandro the other day and I said to him that we have to get together to produce something, to give something back. The key of life is flow, and if you don't make things flow, they die. You have to make your experiences go beyond yourself and count for other people.

ÁNGELES CASTRO: During the hardest, most barren periods of production – and amongst these periods I include the here and now – the film schools are the one sector making films. Some of them may be short films but, still, the schools are the only ones consistently producing. Thanks to the short film festival we organize, there are now many people making shorts, and there is an audience ready and willing to see Mexican short films.

I also think that we have so much that we will contribute to the future of Mexican cinema and in all fields: directing, writing, cinematography. And my hope is that there will be several cross-over breakthroughs of CCC students in the coming years.

GAEL GARCÍA BERNAL: I don't want to be too pessimistic. We have very good foundations in terms of talent, and little by little there are others coming through. The more difficult it is for new film talents to get through, quite often the stronger those talents are. Film may not be high on the agenda for the Mexican government right now – and remember that Vicente Fox's term finishes in a few years – because they see it purely in business terms. But, as a medium, film transcends this. It is through cinema that we learn about other countries and other cultures. And that, after all, is the reason that you and I are talking right now.

Postscript

Since the completion of the writing of this book, various key developments have necessitated the addition of a final chapter to offer an update of the climate in which contemporary Mexican cinema currently finds itself. By looking at the talents that continue to emerge and the developments in the careers of leading Mexican figures, this postscript allows an opportunity to peer, however cautiously, into the future, offering a glimpse of a tantalising and, if various elements hold in place, promising new period in the country's cinematic history.

Despite the unquestionable richness and depth of talent to be found within Mexican filmmaking, the preceding chapter left it facing another of its numerous dark and uncertain moments in the form of President Vicente Fox's would-be purge of state subsides and his plans to axe IMCINE and to close both the famous and talent-breaking Centro de Capacitación Cinematográfica film school (the CCC) and the studios Churbusco. Thankfully, an uproar of dissent prompted the Mexican congress to scrap the proposal but even given the vehemence with which these sanctions were opposed, few people could have predicted the announcement made earlier this year which saw the Mexican Film institute granted the biggest budget allotment from the government in six years.

The state-backed film financing entity was granted a 2004 budget of nearly $14m (150m pesos), more than double last year's budget. With the recent crisis about its future apparently over – though IMCINE director Alfredo Joskowicz is quoted as planning to continue lobbying for tax incentives that would help stimulate private investment as well as find new ways to promote and distribute Mexican cinema abroad – IMCINE now hopes to back a minimum, if a not inconsiderable, 25 films in the coming year. The new budget will be split between the two nearly depleted film funds Fidecine (intended for more mainstream productions) and Foprocine (for directorial debuts and experimental films) with 70m pesos each. The additional 10m pesos will be allotted for short films, a format long supported by the leading film schools within the country and the format through which many of the country's rising crop of young talent forged their distinctive filmmaking styles.

The announcement of increased state support for cinema coincides with a period of continued growth at the Mexican box office for locally produced pictures, proving that the rediscovered appetite for Mexican productions is showing little signs of abating. Directed by Gabriela Tagliavini, *Ladies Night*, the first Mexican feature produced by Disney's Latin American label Miravista, became the Mexican blockbuster of the year with two million admissions in seven weeks. A romantic comedy about two girls who find love in the most unexpected places in modern-day Mexico City, the film currently ranks sixth among the leading Mexican films of all time. 2004 also saw major box office success in Mexico for *Nicotina* (a domestic gross in excess $4m) and Alejandro Lozano's *Matando Cabos*. An offbeat, irreverent and achingly hip comedy about a group of teens in Mexico City, *Matando Cabos* enjoyed an opening box office weekend in excess of $1.3m. Even though poorly received and, for the most part, critically derided Alfonso Arau's costly *Zapata, el sueño del héro*, a biopic of the Mexican Revolutionary Emilano Zapata, still met with relative commercial success, taking over $1.2m on its opening weekend.

Though it is tempting to view 2004 purely in terms of the renewed commitment shown to the Mexican cinema industry by the state and to celebrate the aforementioned local successes as sustained evidence of Mexican cinema's financial force at the box office, it is also equally important, as stated at the outset of this postscript, to give due consideration to the films and filmmakers that are likely to continue the truly international reputation Mexican cinema has come to enjoy. Prominent amongst them is Fernando Eimbcke's *Duck Season* (*Temporada de patos*), a visually and thematically beguiling first feature that is wise and wonderful way beyond its director's tender years. Written by Eimbcke in collaboration with Paula Markovitch, the film also features Felipe Cazals amongst the credits as a script consultant.

Creating a clamour first at Cannes and then at Edinburgh where the film received its UK premiere in August 2004, *Duck Season* evolved out of Eimbcke's desire to make a movie about adolescents that reflected their constant searching and rejection of the established order. Set in the Tlatelolco area of Mexico City, the film opens on a Sunday morning in a run-down council estate with childhood friends Flama (Daniel Miranda) and Moko (Diego Cataño) preparing for a day without parents. Arming themselves with junk food, porn and video games, the pair order pizza and settle down to let the fun begin. Their plans are however interrupted, first by Ulises (Enrique Arreola), the pizza deliveryman who subsequently refuses to leave, and then by Rita (Danny Perea), a voluptuous 16-year-old neighbour who wants to use their oven to bake a cake. Evolving out of this volatile quartet comes a profoundly moving, deceptively simple and ultimately genuine insightful mediation on adolescence, longing, friendship, sexual curiosity and familial strife.

Largely using first time actors and crew and making a virtue of his minimal budget, CCC graduate Eimbcke – who is patently another glowing advertisement for the work the film schools in Mexico are doing and, in this instance, the CCC also funded the film through its script development – keeps the visual aspect of the black and white film uncluttered and simple; something of a surprise given the director's work in music videos. Similarly, the use of music is sparse and the performances deadpan and naturalistic. Little wonder then that the film courted positive comparison to the work of Jim Jarmusch. In aesthetic terms the film is important in that it offers a marked contrast to the similarly themed debut of Alejandro González Iñárritu and Alfonso Cuarón's *Y tu mamá también* and as such provides evidence of the richness and diversity Mexican cinema is capable of producing. Further evidence of a rich and varied tapestry can be found in Juan Carlos Rulfo's *In the Pit* (2006), a Sundance-winning documentary portrait of the construction workers building the second deck of Mexico City's Periferico freeway. An examination of the human dimensions involved in any sizeable public project, it's shot with Rulfo's characteristic eye for beauty.

Alongside the new talent coming through – as represented by *Duck Season* and promising features such as Julián Hernández's *Cielo dividio* (*Broken Sky*) and Julio César Estrada & Estrella Medina Escamilla's *Espinas* (*Thorns*) – it is also essential to note the activities of many of Mexico's more established directors past and present. Since completing *Innocent Voices*, a Salvador-set drama about a young boy who must choose between enlisting in the army or joining the guerrillas, Luis Mandoki is also about to embark on *Amapola*, a political thriller starring Diego Luna. Felipe Cazals, another director whose work stretches back numerous decades, heralded a return to directing with *Digna . . . Hasta el úlimo aliento* (*Digna . . . Worthy to Her Final Breath*). A dramatised feature-length documentary describing the life and work of Mexican lawyer Digna Ochoa y Plácido, Cazals' film was one of numerous titles that screened as part of an enthusiastically received New Mexican Documentaries strand at the Cambridge Film Festival. There have subsequently been a number of similarly related seasons shown throughout the UK, including a retrospective at London's National Film Theatre. Another notable title is the portmanteau picture *Cero y van cuatro*. A gritty crime story that looks at the judicial system in Mexico City, the film pools together the collective talents of Alejandro Gamboa, Antonio Serrano, Carlos Carrera and Fernando Sariñana. It's an uncompromising and grimly realistic work.

Meanwhile, having made an arthouse splash with *Japón*, Carlos Reygadas returned with *Battle in Heaven* (*Batalla en el cielo*), which created a storm at

Cannes. It's another existentialist drama dealing with moral corruption in Mexico City through the relationship between a middle-aged chauffeur (Marcos Hernández) and Ana, the prostitute daughter (Anapola Mushkadiz) of his wealthy boss. When Marcos confesses to Ana his part in the kidnapping of a child that has gone fatally wrong, he sets himself down a path of reckless abandon, climaxing at the Basilica during an intense religious festival in teaming Mexico City. *Battle in Heaven* is an uncompromising vision of human folly – though at the same time, one remarkably open to the possibility of redemption and grace. Cast almost entirely with non-professionals, it's a difficult yet remarkable work that establishes Reygadas as a true visionary of contemporary cinema. Continuing Reygadas' frank exploration of issues relating to sex and sexuality, the film drew words of admiration from luminaries such as González Iñárritu, Alfonso Cuarón and Guillermo del Toro. Reygadas has also taken on a producer's role for other up-and-coming talent. Amat Escalante's *Sangre* is the first fruit of these labours. Escalante was the assistant director on *Battle*

Marcos Hernández and Anapola Mushkadiz in *Battle in Heaven*

in Heaven and his *Sangre* is a similarly virtuoso piece of filmmaking that focuses on an ordinary, middle-aged man's descent into crisis.

Having scored big with *Hellboy* and planning to direct a lucrative sequel, Guillermo del Toro has returned to a project closer to home with the Spanish language *Pan's Labyrinth*. Long time del Toro collaborator Guillermo Navarro serves as director of photography and *Y tu mamá también's* Mirabel Verdú stars. Described by del Toro as 'the single most fulfilling creative experience of my career', it took the director over two years to complete to his satisfaction. The film is a chilling story set against the backdrop of a fascist regime in 1944 rural Spain which focuses on Ofelia, a lonely and dreamy child living with her mother and adoptive father, a military officer tasked with ridding the area of rebels. In her loneliness, Ofelia creates a world filled with fantastical creatures and secret destinies. With post-war repression at its height, Ofelia must come to terms with her world through a fable of her own creation. Alfonso Cuarón cites *Pan's Labyrinth* as 'an explosion of the full potential of Guillermo's mind'.

Alfonso Cuarón – whose brother Carlos is in pre-production on *Toto*, a drama set in the world of professional football starring Diego Luna and Gael García Bernal – has embarked upon a plethora of new productions that echo his personal philosophy that as an artist he should be allowed to work on as international level as possible whilst also remaining true to his Mexican roots. First out of the blocks is *The Children of Men*, a genetics-based sci-fi thriller from the novel by P.D. James. Clive Owen, Julianne Moore and Michael Caine star. *Mexico '68* will deal with the student demonstrations organised against President Díaz Ordaz that saw more than three hundred people massacred by government troops. Cuarón has also announced *The Memory of Running*, the story of an obese Vietnam vet who sets out on a cross-country trip on his bicycle in a bid to reclaim the body of his dead sister. Also in the pipeline is *The History of Love*, a romantic drama based on Nicole Krauss' novel. Cuarón's regular DoP Emmanuel Lubezki – whose other recent credits include *Lemony Snicket's A Series of Unfortunate Events* (2004) and a recent Academy Award nomination for Terrence Malick's *The New World* (2005) – is currently involved in the latter three features

Meanwhile, Alejandro González Iñárritu has re-teamed with regular writing collaborator Guillermo Arriaga for *Babel*, a series of stories set in Morocco, Tunisia, Mexico and Japan that are linked by tragedy and loss. Gael García Bernal, Cate Blanchett and Brad Pitt all star. Straight from the success of Ang Lee's *Brokeback Mountain* (2005), Rodrigo Prieto once again handles cinematographic duties. Gustavo Santaolalla – who won an

Oscar for the music for *Brokeback Mountain* – contributes the score, Brigitte Broch the production design as González Iñárritu retains the creative team that has so far served him so well. *Babel* was selected to screen in competition at the 2006 Cannes Film Festival, as was del Toro's *Pan's Labyrinth*, a notable double whammy for Mexican cinema. The increasingly prolific Arriaga also scripted Tommy Lee Jones' compelling directorial debut *The Three Burials of Melquiades Estrada*. The film, evocative of Sam Peckinpah, continues Arriaga's immersion in the subjects of fate and redemption in an astonishingly perceptive exploration of social and racial injustice in which the body of Mexican immigrant Melquiades Estrada (Cesar Cedillo) is found in a shallow grave in the desert. Making no attempt to solve the crime, the local authorities rapidly transfer the corpse to a pauper's grave. Pete Perkins (a superb, grizzled Lee Jones), Melquiades' best friend, takes it upon himself to track down the murderer and forces him to transport Melquiades to his own personal Eldorado in Mexico, providing his friend with a memorable journey to his third burial. Arriaga appears in a cameo role as a bear hunter. The film offers a non-didactic and heartfelt observation of the current relationship between Mexico and the US.

Finally, what more of Gael García Bernal, the figure who has perhaps become most synonymous with contemporary Mexican cinema and come to symbolise its hopes, dreams and ambitions? A politically committed and independently minded individual who has remained a fiercely passionate advocate of Mexican cinema, the actor carefully nurtured his career after his initial successes, appearing in Spanish language productions such as Walter Salles' *The Motorcycle Diaries* and Pedro Almodóvar's *Bad Education*. He has steadfastly resisted overtures to work in the US, jokingly remarking in a *Time Out* interview that Tijuana was the closest he ever got to Hollywood. Recent projects have seen him continue to resist mainstream Hollywood's charms and lucrative financial rewards for more audacious, challenging fare. *Babel* aside there's *The King*, a brooding, gothic Oedipal drama that marks the fiction debut of British director James Marsh (*Wisconsin Death Trip*). Many other American actors turned down the role García Bernal plays, afraid of the ambiguity the Mexican himself readily embraced. There's also *The Science of Sleep*, French director Michel Gondry's inventive and ambitious take on the relationship between dreams and reality. Claiming that making *The Motorcycle Diaries* reaffirmed his commitment to Latin American cinema (reinforced by his signing up for Argentinean director Hector Babenco's *Pasado, O*), García Bernal recently returned to Mexico where he set up Canana Films, a production company co-owned by Diego Luna. The pair also launched a travelling documentary festival that began in Mexico

City before playing at 16 towns and cities throughout the country. Through Canana, García Bernal will make his directorial debut with *Défecit*, a drama exploring class divisions within Mexico.

And so without wishing to tempt fate, it would seem fairly safe to predict that we may just possibly be approaching an optimistic and opportune moment in Mexican filmmaking. With a renewed sense of commitment towards the arts from the State, a much welcomed degree of financial stability and the continued emergence of new talent to exist alongside more established forces, all the key elements would seem to be in place to ensure that *el cine de Mexico* is now able to compete and excel on both domestic and international levels.

A Note on the Author

Jason Wood is a film programmer and writer. Previous books include *100 American Independent Films* and *Nick Broomfield: Documenting Icons*. His work has also appeared in the *Guardian, Sight and Sound* and *Vertigo*. He is also the co-director of Ion Productions Ltd, an independent filmmaking company.

Acknowledgements

There are so many people to thank for their help and generosity during the writing of this book that it is almost impossible to know where to begin. As good a place as any is with Will Clark and Danny Perkins of Optimum Releasing, the UK distributors of *Amores Perros, The Devil's Backbone* and *Duck Season*, who helped initiate the project. At the earliest stages of research – and during many of the later stages too – I would not have got by without the advice and assistance of Rosa Bosch.

One of the greatest pleasures this book afforded was the opportunity to visit Mexico City to meet with a good deal of the people interviewed herein. During my time there, Bertha Navarro, Martha Sosa, Susana López Aranda and Claudia Prado were particularly accommodating, helping to facilitate meetings and establish new contacts. Prior to my departure Paul Julian Smith provided a sense of local history and recommendations of the best (and cheapest) restaurants. Anna Marie de la Fuente was a further excellent source of industry connections.

Back in the UK, I would like to offer my gratitude to Linda Pariser and to Eva Tarr Kirkhope and Melanie Crawley of the Latin American Film Festival; Susanne Noble of Icon Film Distribution and Cally Gordon of Cally Gordon and French. Eileen Anipare and Sam Richard provided translations. Gavin and Marcus Whitfield were invaluable in regard to sourcing research materials and Michael Leake and Roger Beaumont provided similarly precious technical support. Marc Allenby, Michael Salu and Miguel Ángel Ortega (IMCINE) are whom I have to thank for stills assistance.

I would of course also like to express my sincere gratitude to all those interviewed in this book for so generously giving me their time and for taking an interest in my endeavours. Perhaps most of all I would like to thank Walter Donohue and Richard T. Kelly at Faber and Faber for their skill, patience and trust. Thanks also to Lesley Felce and Jill Burrows at Faber.

My final appreciations are extended to my long-suffering wife Nicky and to my two sons, Felix and Rudy. I dedicate this book to all three of them.

JASON WOOD

Bibliography

Books

Arriaga, Guillermo, *Amores Perros* (original screenplay), Faber and Faber, 2001
—, *A Sweet Scent of Death*, Faber and Faber, 2002
—, *21 Grams* (original screenplay), Faber and Faber, 2003
Berg, Charles Ramírez, *Cinema of Solitude: A Critical Study of Mexican Film, 1967–1983*, University of Texas Press, 1992
Elena, Alberto, and Marina Díaz López (eds.), *The Cinema of Latin America*, Wallflower Press, 2003
Fisher, John (writer and researcher), *The Rough Guide to Mexico*, Penguin, 2003
Mora, Carl J., *Mexican Cinema: Reflections of a Society 1896–1988*, University of California Press, rev. edn, 1989
Paranaguá, Paulo Antonio (ed.), *Mexican Cinema*, BFI Publishing, 1995
Queirós, Eça de, *El crimen del padre Amaro* (novel), Carcanet, 2002
Shaw, Deborah, *Contemporary Cinema of Latin America, 10 Key Films*, Continuum, 2003
Smith, Paul Julian, *Amores Perros* (BFI Modern Classic), BFI Publishing, 2003

Articles

Archibald, David, 'Insects and Violence' (interview with Guillermo del Toro), *Guardian*, 28 November 2001
Brooks, Xan, 'First Steps in Latin', *Guardian*, 19 July 2002
Brown, Colin, 'Children of the Cine Revolucíon', *Screen International*, 19 September 2003
Fuente, Anna Marie de la, 'New Mexico', *Screen International*, 22 February 2002
—, 'World box office focus: Mexico', *Screen International*, 7 March 2003
—, 'Thunder over Mexico', *Screen International*, 14 March 2003
—, 'Latin Revolution: Country Focus Mexico', *Screen International*, 19 September 2003
Kuhn, Kimberly, 'What is a Ghost?: An Interview with Guillermo del Toro', *Cineaste*, spring 2002
Macnab, Geoffrey, 'Revolution in the bedroom', *Independent*, 22 March 2002
Malcolm, Derek, 'Mexico lit up by dog's star', *Observer*, 7 April 2002
Martinez, Jose, 'The Other Conquest', Venice, April 2000
'Mexico's IMCINE is granted $14m budget', staff reporters in Los Angeles, *Screen Daily*, 28 January 2004

Mulkern, Cindy, 'Target Practice', *Hollywood Reporter*, 16–22 May 2000

Sutter, Mary, 'Southern neighbour of U.S. making cinematic waves', *Variety*, 19 May 2002

Tuckman, Jo, 'Boom Goes the Bang', *Guardian*, 20 June 2003

—, 'Studio sell-off may let Hollywood say hasta la vista to Mexican cinema', *Guardian*, 14 November 2003

Index

Where the middle name is a family surname as in Alejandro González Iñárruti the entry will be filed under that name.

Illustrations are entered in **bold**

Index